The Next Chapter

Making Peace

with Hard Memories,

Finding Hope All Around Me,

and Clearing Space for

Good Things to Come

Jana Kramer

The Next Chapter

HarperOne

An Imprint of HarperCollinsPublishers

This is a work of nonfiction. The events and experiences detailed
herein are all true and have been faithfully rendered to the best of my
ability. Some circumstances have been changed in order to protect the
integrity and/or anonymity of the various individuals involved. Though
conversations come from my keen recollection of them, they are not
written to represent word-for-word documentation; rather, I've retold
them in a way that evokes the real feeling and meaning of what was said,
in keeping with the true essence of the mood and spirit of the event.

HarperCollins books may be purchased for educational, business,
or sales promotional use. For information, please email the
Special Markets Department at SPsales@harpercollins.com.

FIRST EDITION

Illustrations © Shutterstock, Inc.

Library of Congress Cataloging-in-Publication Data has been applied for.

ISBN 978-0-06-328869-0

23 24 25 26 27 LBC 5 4 3 2 1

*To my Jolie and Jace, who motivate me to be
the best version of myself*

Contents

Contents

PART THREE
Winter

PART FOUR
Spring

Preface

I was in the downstairs master closet with my two children, Jolie and Jace, one kid huddled under each arm. Tornado sirens were going off all over Nashville. Tonight would be a disaster. Just north of us in Kentucky, a tornado was supposed to touch down and tear through a small town. For all we knew, it was headed our way next.

I didn't hesitate, my fingers moving to the only name in my contact list I knew to call.

"Hi," I said a little shakily, just as My Ex picked up.

"Jana," he said. "Are you and the kids in the safe spot?"

"Yes." I felt better instantly, as I knew I would.

We had signed divorce papers a year ago, so why would I call the man who I was 100 percent certain had ruined my life? The man I blamed for breaking up my family? The man whose cheating and lying was a permanent blemish on my career?

You might wonder why I didn't call anyone else.

I called because I was scared. In fact, I was terrified. In moments like this, My Ex was our rock. He was my anxiety blanket, and I trusted that he would have the answers and that he would protect the kids and me like he always did in the past. This wasn't the first time a tornado siren had gone off and we huddled as a family in a closet. But, this time, our foursome was down to three. I felt the ex-husband-sized hole at that moment, and I know the kids did too.

Jolie, Jace, and I still lived in the house where our marriage played out. It was the place where My Ex and I got back together after his first infidelity came to light six years earlier and where we vowed to try again. It's where we fell apart once more, doubled down on our commitment, renewed our vows, wrote a book about the experience, and celebrated its success and our own. It's also where we had our last fight, and, finally, where I signed the divorce paperwork a year later, just down the hall from where I sat huddled in the closet now.

As the kids fought for the phone, hoping to hear their dad's voice, I held on. I was silent, and so was he. I wondered if he wished he was there with us. I let that thought arrive, and then I let it pass.

"It's really eerie out," he said.

"It is . . ."

There was so much more I wanted to say, but instead, I said, "I'm scared."

"You're okay. Just stay in the closet," he said.

✳   ✳   ✳

So much went wrong between My Ex and me. Our marriage suffered from the same issues that plague many relationships (believe me, I receive more direct messages confirming this than I could possibly count), but our suffering was for the world to see. My Ex's sex addiction and recovery, followed by a series of relapses, was covered widely by the media. We never shied away from discussing our problems or our decision to stay together, so when the marriage fell apart, the shame was immense and all-consuming. I was cast as the eternal victim, and he, the perpetrator. These two roles neither captured who we really were nor gave us a chance to evolve beyond them.

After the divorce was finalized, I had to face the failure of the longest relationship I had ever been in. I suffered financially, as I had to spend almost half my money on a settlement, legal fees, and child support for My Ex. It was also the first time I was separated from my children since they were born.

"Will you stay on the phone with us until it passes?"

"Of course," he said.

At that moment I wanted the four of us to be together. I wanted to say I wished he was with us. But I didn't. I left it out for a good reason. There was no use treading old ground or bonding over trauma. There was no use stating the obvious. There was no going back now. He knew that, and I knew that too. A silent understanding.

"Tonight scared me too." He paused, then said, "And it made me miss my family."

I knew he meant it, that he felt the same emptiness that we did. Somehow, this realization that we each felt the other's

absence and could admit it without desiring physical close-
ness confirmed that there wasn't a drop of romantic love
left between us. But there was a chance now for something
even better: respect, consistency, kindness, forgiveness, and
growth.

As I looked at Jolie and Jace, giggling and smiling now that
their dad was on the line, the closet experience now feeling
more like a game than a desperate attempt at safety, I could see
that clearly much went right between My Ex and me too. That
was undeniable: My kids are perfection, and they were raised
with love all around them. Although that love had fizzled out
in My Ex's heart and mine, it still lived in them.

After another moment, the sirens stopped. We all said
goodbye and hung up. Then the kids and I, exhausted and
ready for sleep, emerged from the closet.

There are truths and lies in every relationship story, and
they are impossible to capture accurately from just one perspective. My relationship with My Ex (who I refer to as "My
Ex" throughout this book to keep things simple, protect
his privacy, and hopefully make it clear that this story isn't
about him, but me) is a tangled mess of memories, experiences, dreams, sacrifices, and compromises.

I don't claim to be able to tell you what to do with your own
relationships. I can barely make sense of my own at times, let
alone know what could be going on with yours. When I wrote
my first book, *The Good Fight*, with My Ex, I thought I knew

what was best when it came to relationships. In the book, we wrote about what we went through to save our relationship, but the truth is, some of the choices I made weren't really in line with how I felt. Looking back, I can see how I was trying to convince myself that the work we were doing was helping our relationship, and that I was making decisions that were in line with my best interests. I thought if our story helped other people, that our issues would just magically go away or wouldn't look as bad. Problem was, the more we tried to help others, the more depressed we became, knowing we were still struggling and our relationship was not getting better.

These days, I only know the truth of my own life. I see the details clearer, examine them with more compassion, and am confident in my ability to choose next steps for myself in a way I never did before or when I was married to My Ex. I am confident only in *myself* these days—in my path, my quiet reflection, my God, my stillness, and my ability to give and feel joy.

This book is meant to capture a year of these details of my life—how I moved from signing divorce papers in a state of hysteria and devastation to sitting in a closet with my kids during a tornado siren, on the phone with My Ex, feeling satisfied in the knowledge that we had no more storms to fight.

This book isn't a tell-all about a failed marriage, nor is it a how-to guide to relationships. It is not meant to advise you to take the same actions I did, but to show you how I evolved over the course of a year—sometimes for the better, sometimes not.

I also discovered that the seemingly opposing feelings of

loss and liberation can exist at the same time. I do hope this book helps you see that while the loss of something may cause pain and create wreckage in your life, it can also make you feel lighter and freer as you work through it. They say a person grips the tightest before letting go, and boy did I ever. But the joy on the other side of letting go is worth it. I've found that to be true in my life, and I believe it can be true in yours.

Introduction

It's Over

In February 2021, My Ex, our two children, and I were spending a little over a month in Vancouver, Canada, where I was filming a movie. COVID-19 mandates were still in place and a two-week quarantine was enforced by the Canadian government and production. We were in lockdown, forced to spend every moment together on the property. We had a tracking app on our phone that made sure we stayed on the property of the house, and food was delivered to the door. So we became a four-person bubble.

We were staying in a precious farmhouse on a property lined with beautiful trees. I remember seeing the place on Airbnb and falling in love with its rustic yet cozy feeling. I thought, "Now this is where we'll make some great family memories." Little did I know that the only memories I would have from that trip would be spilled Cheerios all over the floor, slammed doors, sleepless nights—and a painting of a cow. We'll get to the cow in a minute.

My Ex and I traveled a lot for work, and we were always good about making every new place we stayed feel like a home. But not this time. We tried. Boy, did we try, but no amount of trying could solve our problems. We were both frayed from COVID fears, and frustrations about our marriage were at a boil; by the time we got to this "tranquil Vancouver vacation home for a family," there was no chance the place would feel like a home, despite our usual efforts. The description of the place was spot on, but the walls of our marriage were crumbling, and there was no fixing them now.

One night during our second week at the house, my husband was upstairs, stomping around out of anger. We had just had a fight. Our Zoom couple's session had gone south. Looking back, quarantine in Canada seems like a cruel joke we were playing on one another: we were isolated and on the brink of a meltdown for two weeks while we insisted on continuing our couples therapy sessions on Zoom. What were we thinking?

This fight was about a five-hundred-dollar watch My Ex had just bought. I had become angry about the number of boxes arriving at the house, and the new hobbies he was picking up that were costing us a lot of money. I come from a scarcity mindset, a childhood where we didn't have much, and I have the type of career where recurring paychecks are a long time coming. Seeing money fly out of our accounts in a time of so much uncertainty, in addition to the fact that neither one of us worked steadily the previous year, was really making me panic. We needed to rein in the spending, so we had agreed to go on a budget. The problem was, only one of us stuck to it.

Here is how the Zoom conversation went after I confronted My Ex about the watch:

"What does it matter?" he asked, getting defensive.

I said, "It matters because, yet again, you can't respect one boundary that we set in place."

"It was a watch for five hundred dollars. Big deal, Jana."

"I get that, but the budget was something we set up to do together. By you not following the plan, once again it feels like you aren't respecting me."

Our therapist, his head moving back and forth as if he were watching a tennis match on TV, observed the fight in silence. I didn't need the therapist's help in deducing My Ex's motives, though. I was hip to why he did what he did at that point. The watch buying was just another metaphor for his resentment of feeling controlled. The budget only highlighted the fact that he felt he was in a cage, without freedom. Meanwhile, I was begging for respect, dependability, and teamwork in our relationship.

It wasn't long before My Ex stood up abruptly, left the room where we were having the session in a fury, and slammed the door behind him, leaving our therapist and me staring at each other in silence. I felt so alone in that tiny space, especially with our therapist three thousand miles away. I was so embarrassed; I could barely look up at the screen long enough to hit "end call."

"Now what?" I thought. My Ex didn't want me to follow him. I knew he wanted nothing to do with me. His hiding spot was in the spare room, along with his iPad, so I assumed that's where he had fled. Our two children were asleep down the hall. I would have to be up before sunrise tomorrow to be on set. I should've been sleeping, but I couldn't go upstairs. I couldn't go for a walk. I couldn't take a bath, clean the counter, or watch TV. I walked to the living room, where I had found the only solace I could find in this house the last two weeks.

I was staring at the cow again. All I could do was stare at this damn cow.

Let me back up.

My Ex and I were no strangers to fighting. In fact, we had just released our bestselling book *The Good Fight*, which was about how to make a relationship work after infidelity, lying, and broken trust—which My Ex and I had done successfully. My Ex had cheated on me throughout the first year of our six-year marriage before I discovered the infidelities and was forced to upend the entire structure of our relationship. After all, we had a daughter, we were a family, and we still had love. My Ex went to rehab for sex addiction, got a sponsor, and stuck to a program. We worked through the issues together. We worked through relapses, deceit, and exhausting hours of therapy during recovery. It was a painful but incredible and life-changing experience to stay together when so many people would have ended the relationship. We did the work with compassion for each other and made it to the other side. We had broken the mold in that way. We were walking examples of hard work in our decision to stay together. More important, our ability to help other couples do the same made both of us proud. Ours was a story of redemption and hope, and we took the responsibility of helping other couples very seriously.

Why, then, was I staring at this painting of a cow in the living room? Why wasn't I upstairs practicing what I was preaching in that book of ours—fighting with boundaries, communicating, and listening? Why wasn't he doing the same?

I knew that if I went upstairs, I would be met with the same patronizing, mean, hurtful version of the man I married. No, I couldn't go upstairs. A voice had started to whisper to me. Yes, I know how that sounds. I heard it loudest when I was staring at this stunning painting of a brown-and-white cow that hung on the wall of the living room. She had big, beautiful eyes and a serene confidence. That's why I kept coming back to her, to hear that voice, the voice said, "Wake up, wake up, wake up."

◦   ◦   ◦

Vancouver had been a mess from the start. I had been keeping a journal about our relationship. I would write down the details of every day to help me determine whether we had a good day or a bad one. Literally. That might sound like an extreme way to evaluate a relationship, but I had to do something because I had started to question my sanity. I was busy. I was working. I was stressed out. I was coming home exhausted and feeling worse by the time bedtime rolled around. Seeing the day written out in black and white on paper helped me make sense of things.

Most days were summed up with one word: "bad."

I felt like a prisoner with no chance of escape. Each night, when it seemed I had no choice but to confront my husband about our lack of consistency or mutual loneliness, or his self-ishness or my selfishness, I would find my way to the painting of the cow. I'm not sure what pulled me to her. I like art as much as the next human with a heart, but this response was different from anything I had experienced before. Who was behind those eyes? I felt a spiritual connection I was desperate for when I looked at the painting, as if the cow's eyes were speaking to my soul, and my soul was speaking back. Quarantine in Vancouver had me talking to a cow. We can all laugh at that.

I remember the sad truth of how I was feeling when I was talking to "Lucy" (yes, I named her). I was lonely. I felt hatred from my husband, and I was worried about how that hatred would affect my children and me. I questioned whether I had hatred growing in my heart too. The days were bad and getting worse, and that's when the voice was the strongest.

"Wake up, wake up, wake up."

"Jana, it's over."

But I wasn't ready.

• • •

A few months after Vancouver, I was recovering from a breast augmentation at home in Nashville. I was still in a lot of pain, and I had a lot of physical limitations. I couldn't lift anything heavier than ten pounds. In the bedroom, my laundry basket was filling up and getting heavier by the day. Finally, I started to drag and push it toward the door to move it to the laundry room. My Ex noticed what I was doing and offered to do my laundry.

This was a tough moment for me. In our relationship, I struggled to ask for help because when I did, he didn't come through. I hesitated, but then decided to ask, to put into practice what my therapist had been telling me to do for the better part of a decade.

"That would mean a lot," I said. "But if you could, please do it as soon as possible as I really need this surgical bra."

"Not a problem. I'll do it in the morning," he said.

Fast forward to five o'clock the next afternoon: my clothes were still sitting in the hamper. I really needed this bra, but I didn't want to push him, to try to control the situation. My feelings were bouncing back and forth between anger and disappointment. I kept saying to myself, "He said he would do it." Finally, at seven, I went into the laundry room, and found my clothes, still wet, in the washing machine.

I left the laundry room to go to the bedroom, and that's when I really processed my surroundings. The house was in complete disarray. There were delivered boxes in the foyer that needed to be opened. In the kitchen, food was on the counter, and utensils, plates, and cups were strewn about. The living room looked like there had been an explosion of kids' toys and electronics. Throughout the house, it felt like everything had been left out for me to deal with.

I walked into our bedroom and sat on the bench there. My Ex and I were supposed to spend time together that night, to have one of our "intentional nights"—connecting and being present with each other with no phones or distractions—that we talk about in *The Good Fight*.

He said, "Are you ready to hang?"

I was tired and annoyed once again. I thought to myself, "See, this is why you don't ask for help." I looked up and gave a dismissive "sure," which ignited My Ex. His response: "What's your issue now?"

Once again, we began to argue, to do the passive and defensive verbal dance that we did so well that we could have patented it. After going around and around in our usual draining circles, I tried to end the conversation.

"I'm really bummed out that something I asked you to do wasn't followed through with," I said.

He replied, "I didn't know you were such a fucking cripple."

I said nothing. Defeated, I got up and walked to the laundry room. I could hear his footsteps behind me, though. Of course, he was following me. Of course, he couldn't just apologize and admit wrongdoing. We also had a knack for not giving each other space when things got heated.

He stormed into the room, opened the washer, and started to throw the wet laundry at me, saying, "Here are your fucking clothes." In trying to avoid being hit by the wadded-up wash my six-foot-five, two-hundred-and-fifty-pound husband kept hurling at me, I lost my balance and fell. Against my will, I started to cry.

In true Ex fashion he said, "That didn't hurt. Get the fuck up."

I stood up. In the past, I would have fought back and got in his face, but when I turned around to face him, I had no fight left. I looked him right in the eyes, but I found I had nothing to say. Instead, I ran to the guest room closet. It had become a familiar place I would find myself going to, to escape the reality of my situation. I often prayed that it would turn into a magical doorway that would lead me to a different time and place. I could hear My Ex storming around the house calling my name and saying, "Oh, boohoo. Go fucking cry." That was his superpower: mocking me. And this was my superpower: hiding, wishing, and dreaming for some other outcome to our problems rather than the same old results.

I debated my next steps. Do I find him and apologize for overreacting and being upset that my laundry wasn't done? Do I say nothing but have my body language be passive so he knows I am mad? Do I try to see if he can see my pain and empathize? Do I try to get an apology out of him that I know, or I think, I deserve? I sat there pondering my next step and replaying all the times I tried those things—and that they never worked. At that moment, though, I felt something I never felt before. I heard the same voice I heard in my heart a year ago in Vancouver. That whisper. A year ago, I wasn't strong enough to end things. I would have marched into our bedroom, kicked him out, and we would have done the same dance that we always did. I would have fought to have him see why he hurt me. But today, all I could see before me were the manipulations, little insecurities, and grievances at play like moves on a chessboard.

It was then that I realized I had lost the purpose of why I was staying to play this game. I didn't want to be married to this man anymore. I didn't want to have clothes thrown at me or to be ridiculed. I didn't want to be hiding in a closet in my own home from someone who is supposed to love me. I didn't like how I felt—the heaviness of it all. I was sure as hell he didn't want to be married to me either.

I was sure he hated me. I used to ask him all the time why

he hated me. He never had a good answer, but I think he hated himself too. He created a giant black hole in our marriage that we both couldn't get out of. At that moment, sitting in a dark closet, I had the greatest revelation of my life: Staying would hurt worse than leaving. I wanted out.

When My Ex gave up on the search-and-fight mission and the house was quiet, I opened the closet door and I crawled into the guest room bed to sleep. I prayed these simple words: "God, please just slap me in the face with it."

And boy, did he ever.

That next morning, the house was quiet. Jolie was at school, and My Ex had taken Jace to a play space for kids. I had no messages on my phone, no "I'm sorry for throwing clothes at you." Nothing. That wasn't unusual, though. He would always start a fight by blaming me for the way I reacted to things. And for me I would struggle with saying I was sorry because the affairs were always the underlying stem of our fights. I had a harder time looking at myself because what he did was always worse. With most of our explosive fights, it would take two to three days before he would apologize genuinely for his part, and life would pick up again. Something about this day felt different, though, like a bomb was being lit.

I walked into our bedroom and decided to check his iPad. I went to his email and looked in the trash folder. Nothing. I went to the inbox. Nothing. Then I put the iPad down and looked out the window. It was almost as if I *wanted* to find something. I wanted a reason to get out; I was so tired of the life I was living. I looked down at the iPad and then clicked on sent messages. There it was. My reason. I found emails to another woman, sent from an account I had no knowledge of.

(Here's a lesson for those trying to hide things: don't forget to delete your sent messages.)

I immediately texted "911" to my best friend, Kathryn. She knew what that meant. Within less than an hour we were sitting together on a bench in the bedroom, waiting for My Ex to come home. The laptop lay on the unmade bed.

When I heard him walk in, my heart started to beat faster. I looked over to Kathryn and gave her one last look for strength and took a deep breath as I heard his footsteps rounding the corner.

"What is this?" he asked as he entered the room.

I looked at Kathryn and then at him. I said, "I need you to log into your fake email account."

He replied, "I don't have a fake email account. I'm sorry you feel that way."

I stared at him. At that moment, I just felt sad. Like, here we are again. Here I am sitting in front of my husband and being lied to again, for the one-hundredth, maybe two-hundredth time.

"Get out," I said calmly.

He was out of plays. He was caught and he knew it. He didn't move. He just stood there staring at me.

I said it again, a little more forcefully.

And then I said it again, this time even louder, "Get out!"

Once he left, Kathryn asked if she should call the lawyers or whether I was going to do that. I told her I needed some time to think. I could see the disappointment in her eyes.

It is hard to explain what happened over the next few days,

except that what went down was just more of the same. There were tears. He apologized for sending inappropriate messages to other women, swearing up and down that nothing physical had happened. That the fake email account was something he never ended up using. I pretended that I already knew everything and that I had direct messages to prove it, which drew out a bit more "truth" from him, even after he swore he'd told me everything. This time, I had the upper hand, although I never knew what to do with it when I had it. Having the upper hand was better than being derided and having my feelings minimized. But, was it better, really? When My Ex had the upper hand, he was cruel; when I had it, I felt disgusted and paralyzed because it meant that I would be lied to and gaslit again. These seemed to be my only two options for handling the problems in our marriage and they both made me feel so dead inside. Why were these my only two options?

Alongside a voice of reason was a voice of shame: we were *New York Times* bestselling authors of a book on saving a marriage. We even had another book—on trust!—signed up. We were the couple that could fight through anything, right? I felt like I was trapped in an open sea, just flailing my arms around. I was sinking. I had no life jacket, and there was no lifeboat coming my way. Did I mention I can't swim? Can't anyone see me out here? Surely y'all could? Now, when I look at archived stories on Instagram, I can see I was dying inside. Hell, I can see My Ex was too. We were both crying for an out with our filtered smiles.

Meanwhile, he said all the things he always did. He didn't want me to leave, he wanted to make this work. He would never do it again. He truly had hit rock bottom—could I just give him one more chance? He was an addict, and he was getting better.

He even went as far as to tell me things he did during our marriage that I didn't know about—to maybe garner some trust with me and to show me he was capable of being honest with himself. I asked him if there were any other truths he needed to tell me about my recent findings.

He said, "I have never been so honest in my life. There is absolutely nothing else, I promise."

My gut knew better, so I dug in one last time.

The next day, after a night of crying and yelling and crying, he revealed that he physically cheated on me while he was working on his problems at a therapy retreat center more than a year earlier.

He was so sorry. It would never happen again.

This time was different. I didn't have tears to cry. I didn't yell at him at that moment. I already knew in my gut that he had cheated again. I just needed him to admit it. You see, I had heard a whisper of a way out of this situation back in Vancouver, and the whisper started in my own head and heart.

Despite all the obvious hurt of the cheating and lying, I couldn't shake the laundry room incident most of all. At that moment, the whisper became a scream. I could see that none of this was about me. My Ex was always going to end up in a laundry room somewhere, throwing wet clothes at the person he claimed to love. He was always going to belittle her and rationalize his actions to make himself feel better about the lies he lives in his dysfunctional double life.

But I didn't need to end up in that laundry room with him. Everything clicked for me in the laundry room—I *needed* to wake up. This was a cycle that was never going to end for him or us. However, it could end for me.

I didn't leave our marriage seven years earlier when I found out about the first round of affairs because we had just had our daughter, our sweet Jolie Rae. I couldn't imagine another woman being around my daughter or another woman getting the better, reformed version of my husband after he destroyed me. I didn't want someone else to get the version I deserved, so after My Ex's every relapse, I held on to the hope that he would be the man he promised me he would be. This time though, he could have promised me the world and I couldn't have cared less. "The next woman can have him," I thought. I didn't want the changed man anymore. I had enough of all versions.

A few days later, Kathryn came over. She knew that this last event was about more than just the latest round of cheating messages and information. She said quietly, "Jana, you've got your smoking gun."

I filed divorce papers that day.

• • •

I wish that I could tell you that from that moment on I was resolute. But the truth is, I was holding out for any small sign from God. I realize God had just hit me with a Mack truck, but I was thinking, "Well, maybe, just maybe, there will now be a sign to stay." I kept thinking about my babies and all the times I wouldn't be with them if the divorce went through. I kept thinking how unfair that was. My kids would not be with me full-time—any moment without them would be an injustice too great to accept. I admit I looked for signs to stay so I would never have to pack my kids' clothes and say, "See you tomorrow when you come home from Daddy's house."

I called two of our old couples' therapists and told them what happened. They were disappointed in the recent discoveries, but they didn't sound that surprised. They reminded me of instances when My Ex would struggle with empathy or exhibit bad behavior, like the time he nearly flipped over the coffee table in one of their offices out of rage. Those stories brought me back to all the times the therapists tried to open my eyes to the truth.

Then there was my conversation with one of my pastors. He told me stories of redemption and of marriages that survived infidelity. He reminded me that the Bible says, "If God could restore us back to himself, he can restore any relationship back to us," and "It's God's will to bring everything together in Christ."

Stay with me, this is where it gets good.

I had to confront the biggest question of my life: Where was God in all of this? Was he in those lines in the Bible telling me to stay and forgive? Or was he that little voice in my heart telling me to wake up?

I didn't want to believe what I already knew was the truth. I'll repeat that. I didn't want to believe what *I already knew* was the truth. Because that's the thing. You know the truth. I knew the truth. We always know the truth. We just can't prove it. Even deeper, we don't *want* to believe it.

My good friend Lysa Terkeurst once said to me, "We all meet our maker." What she meant is that we all must face the truth of who we are. When I talk about "truth," I'm referring to our inner voice, the voice that has always been there, the voice that gives us direction on our life's path, if we will only listen to it. The more you trust yourself, the more you trust the situation.

• • •

A week after My Ex left, I sat in my lawyer's office, feeling as if someone died. I felt out of body; her mouth was moving but I heard nothing she said. We needed to serve My Ex the divorce papers, but I had no idea where he was staying. I said I would invite him over to put the kids to bed and that we could have someone waiting outside the house to serve him.

The day came. Pamelyn, my best friend and neighbor who lives four doors down, kept watch in front of her house. Kathryn sat in my living room. And me? I was in my bedroom, hysterical.

The plan was that My Ex would put the kids to bed, then when he left the house, a man hired by my lawyer would serve him the divorce papers—and that was going to be that. The end of my happily ever after. The end of my life as I knew it. The end of my perfect family for my kids.

I wailed in my room. I felt like an addict; it was as if my drug dealer was in the house, and I was begging for him to give me a hit. That's how loud I was crying. The painful truth is that I wanted My Ex to come in. I needed that fix. I wanted the pain to go away. I wanted him to hold me, to tell me everything was going to be okay. That he would never hurt me again. That it was all just a bad dream. I heard him walking toward the bedroom, then stop when Kathryn told him not to come in. I could hear him say he wanted to see me and say sorry because he could hear the cries but Kathryn pleaded and begged for him to just leave and not go in there.

Kathryn was my angel that day, protecting me from my drug. If My Ex had walked into that room, I don't know where I would be now. The second he left the house he was served the papers, then Kathryn walked into the room and said, "It's done."

No one can tell me there wasn't a death because that's how it felt. Within a few minutes I posted on Instagram that we were divorcing. I knew that if I didn't put the news out there right then, I would have let My Ex come back in, somehow, some way. If I put it out there, then there would be no way I could take it back. How could I? I would have looked like a fool, yet again. I hit post, then cried and prayed myself to sleep.

I guess it's just so clear that at a certain time in life you must surrender to God for him to do what he has intended us to do with our lives.

- - -

"I want you to try to forget the cheating. Forget the affairs. Forget the lies. All that stuff is so big it is like a thunderstorm you can't see through or past. If you can forget all that stuff and look at him honestly, Jana, you might admit that you didn't really like him."

That's a direct quote from my therapist in one of our sessions a few days after My Ex and I split up. I look up to my therapist so much. I have been doing therapy for years, but

I've never truly connected to someone the way I do with her. She was on this up-and-down journey with me for three years, as I came in and out of her office, asking whether I should get a divorce, and what to do. Obviously, she could never tell me what to do, but looking back now, I can see how she would try to help me listen to my feelings and find my direction.

Once we were doing an exercise with these therapeutic cards with pictures and emotion-related words and she asked, "In your marriage right now, how do you feel?"

The words "sad," "lonely," and "numb" were just a few of the cards I grabbed from the pile. Then she told me to pick cards that represented where I wanted to be. The words "free," "safe," and "happy" filled the cute art deco rug that lined the floors.

She looked at the second set of cards and asked, "How do we get to this side?"

After years of watching the same car crash over and over again, I'm sure as a person she wanted me to say "walk away," but as my therapist in the sessions, she always directed me to focus on me, not my relationship with My Ex. The work we did was about getting me healthy, happy, and strong enough to know what I deserve and don't.

My therapist was the second call I made after I discovered My Ex's last round of affairs. Her words pierced me, then she helped me get strong enough to do what I always knew I had to do. In our session the week the divorce was finalized, we wore black. We had a funeral for my marriage, and I read a eulogy to say goodbye. We lit a candle, and I buried my marriage in that office.

When she mentioned that I didn't like My Ex, I froze. I'm rarely speechless but I remember tilting my head and pausing to let what she said to me really sink in. It was hard to do, and I'll tell you why. I believed all our marital issues were due to the affairs and the lies. These things were the cancer that was destroying our marriage. Grabbing a hold of every memory. It was the white elephant gift that kept on giving. I pondered that question as I sat there in her safe, fireplace-lit office with a weighted blanket and an herbal tea.

That idea was the greatest lie of our relationship: If there weren't epic infidelity issues, we would be the happiest, most loving couple, all sunshine and butterflies. It was the lie we told ourselves during every fight and every time we made up. It was the lie we brought into every happy moment as well, as if life would have been easy and great if we could *just get over this one thing*.

I remember a trip we took to Cabo in October 2020 to celebrate our book becoming a *New York Times* bestseller. I was so excited to be with My Ex, especially after almost a year of being cooped up in a house with two kids and getting through the fights we had during our book tour. We needed it. I needed it. I think I had fantasized about how romantic this trip was going to be—how he was going to rip my clothes off and be passionate with me. How we would stare at the stars to the sound of crashing ocean waves as we leaned into intimate, loving conversations.

One night in Cabo, as I heard the mariachi band playing while we sat semi-quietly over our grilled sea bass and guaca-mole, I asked him to dance. Why not? I wanted to have *fun* with my husband. He said no. That's the thing about having expectations or, shall I say, hope. I set myself up for disappointment because, in truth, we never had that level of romance in our relationship. Maybe in the beginning we had a few passionate nights, but I was never touched or seen the way I longed to be. He used to say, "Nothing is ever good enough for you." And I often wondered if he was right. *Maybe it's just me. Maybe I do ask for too much. Or maybe I was just asking the wrong person.*

I often wonder what our relationship would have been like if he didn't continue to cheat or ever cheat at all. I always told him I wish I was afforded the opportunity to have been the wife I wanted to be and not the one I became because of the things he did. I wish I got the man he promised me he was. In the end, though, would we have made it if he didn't cheat? I'll never know the answer. I know relationships are hard. They take work. They take time, sacrifice, and patience. But I also don't think a relationship should be as hard as mine was. Of course, I have no idea. All I can say is that if I were to look past the infidelity, the root of all our problems, and look at our marriage more closely, it's obvious my needs weren't being met. The infidelity just highlighted that more.

The impetus to leave doesn't have to come with a big reveal or a massive implosion like I experienced. It can be a single argument or look from your partner that tips the scales and gives you that push of strength to go. My therapist told me a related story in session one day. She said she had a client who was being physically abused by her partner almost daily, yet she was having a hard time ending things. One day, though, the client came in to her session and said, "I'm done, and I'm leaving." My therapist asked her what had happened for her to come to this decision, and the client said, "My husband took a bat to my grandmother's vintage table that I've been restoring since her death." My therapist said, "But he has been beating you every day." The client continued, saying that her grandmother meant the world to her, and her husband knew it. The fact that her husband intentionally hurt her by ruining something that belonged to someone she loved so much was the breaking point. No matter how she got there, this woman finally had the strength to act, to make a very much-needed change, just as I did. We all need to do things our own way and in our own time; if you're struggling in a situation, you will know when the time is right for you too.

▪ ▪ ▪

Before I filed for divorce, My Ex and I had just closed a deal with our publisher to write a book about trust, or more specifically, building back trust in a relationship. We were supposed to write about how to trust a partner again, how to be worthy of trust. After our divorce, I figured I would never write another book. How could I possibly try to write again when my first book would always be there as this physical example of everything I had gotten wrong? As it turns out, I was meant to write a book about trust all along, but I was meant to write it alone. Over the last two years, I have become an expert in next chapters. In moving on. In choosing myself.

Instead of trusting your partner, this is a book about trusting yourself. Trusting what's around the corner in your life.

Trusting God. Trusting your next chapter is going to hold exactly what you need.

For me, my divorce was a monumental event that undid my entire life, but this book isn't about divorce. This is a book for anyone who has experienced a huge change or turning point in their life and is figuring out how to rebuild their life. Yes, you will hear about paperwork, custody, and childcare, but I hope you see those details as situational. You have your own circumstances to attend to. It is the effort and the healing that comes with discovering a next chapter that I want to share with you.

I wrote this book a few years after my divorce; the focus is on the single year that followed, when my life shifted in immense ways. In reflecting on that year, I'm trying to bring it into real time through relating specific details and scenes as well as including my journal entries. I needed the space of these last few years to write the book so I could offer a deep and meaningful reflection to make this next chapter worthy of telling, yet, I still feel close to that experience—I can feel the weight of the heartbreak and the turn of the nausea in my stomach. I share that with you too.

All in all, I wrote this to help you know you're not alone on this journey. That though something seems terrifying, and really hard, it's not going to kill you. I made some big changes, ones that I thought would shatter me, but I have found strength on the other side. I hope my story gives you the courage to take a step toward a new path.

part one

Summer

Look Up

Consider it pure joy, my brothers and sisters, whenever you face trials of many kinds, because you know that the testing of your faith produces perseverance.

—JAMES 1: 2–3

2021
May and June

I hardly slept the night I served My Ex the divorce papers. I had a pit in my stomach and tossed and turned, for what I feared had just come true: I was alone. The only thing bringing me comfort was knowing that Kathryn was asleep in the guest room; she had stayed the night so I wouldn't be by myself. When I got out of bed the next morning, my eyes were swollen from crying and I felt that I would get sick at any second and need to run to the toilet. My body was in a state of panic. I couldn't stop shaking. All I wanted to do was crawl back into bed, but instead, I went to get Jolie and Jace ready for school. When I saw their sweet, happy eyes looking at me, I thought, "Just make it to drop off. Then you can cry until pick up."

I went downstairs and started the morning routine: I gave the kids their cereal and made their lunch. Then I played dinosaurs with Jace because he'd been begging for me to play with him since waking up. I sat at the breakfast table with the kids, and I did what all my friends told me not to do: I turned on my phone. I had promised my friends I would delete my Instagram page, and let it sit there for a few days. Somehow, not looking at Instagram made me more anxious. I turned on my phone, and there it was: A photograph of My Ex and me, a broken heart on our image was all over the news, all over Instagram. Everywhere. Over a hundred text messages were on my phone. My heart started to pound, and my breathing became shallow. I was having a panic attack, plain and simple. I could think of nothing but my kids, wondering, "How in the world am I going to be a mother right now?" I got up from the table and made my way out of the kitchen so the kids wouldn't see me lose it. Once I reached the hall, I collapsed on the floor.

Kathryn came out of the guest room and sat beside me. I asked her if she would take my kids to school.

"No," she said flatly. She had turned from kind to cold in an instant.

• • •

Growing up, I was blessed with great friends who cared about me. They were there during some turbulent adolescent years, or when Evan Macomb made fun of me when a tampon fell out of my backpack freshman year. I'll never forget being called to see my eighth-grade counselor because my friends were worried about me: I had told them at lunch that I couldn't eat Oreos. My parents had just gotten divorced, and I do think I was crying out for some attention. They didn't skip a beat to make sure I was okay. Throughout my twenties, I had friends who would come and go. At that stage in my life, it was about having a lot of friends rather than quality friends. In LA, I had my "going out" friends, my "famous" friends, my "brunch, lunch, or coffee" friends, my "that was a wild night last night, can't wait to hear the drama" friends, and my "I just want to lay on the couch and do nothing" friends.

When my life started to change—notably, after getting married and having kids—my circle of friends changed dramatically. The list of people I could rely on started shrinking at a time when I needed support. Not everyone could relate to changing dirty diapers and not being able to go out every night, or even once a week. As my priorities shifted and what I wanted and needed in my friendships came into focus, I started to form friendships more slowly and carefully. I've got a tight group of friends now—we call ourselves the Queendom—and these women have been there for me through all of it.

Chief among my new friend group was Kathryn. When I

was working on *One Tree Hill* in 2012, Kathryn was working for a music management company. She saw me singing on the show and told her boss about me. She flew out to see me on set in North Carolina, and the rest is history. I'll never forget the first time Kathryn and I worked together. We were in a city known for its nightlife, and our day had just wrapped. As we waited for the car to take us to the hotel, Kathryn seemed nervous, and I sensed that she wanted to ask me if I wanted to hang out. I looked at her as if to say, "It's okay, go on," and then she asked, "Do you want to go out to a bar or something?"

Knowing Kathryn as well as I do now, that must have been so hard for her. Sweatpants and staying in are her love languages.

Without skipping a beat, I said, "Hell, no!" and then asked if we could watch some TV instead. In a small hotel, we lay in bed, bonding simply because we both loved the comfort of quiet, cozy spaces and the freedom to be ourselves. Over the next thirteen years, our friendship deepened and Kathryn became like a sister to me. She was the matron of honor in my wedding, and she was, and is, my right hand.

What makes this moment in the hallway extra-meaningful is that Kathryn has stuck with me through everything. She watched me not love myself for years, but never once wavered in her love for me. I can only recall one fight we have ever had. It was right after my breakup with Brantley. I let a good guy go and I knew it. Brantley wanted to give me the world and he went down trying, but nothing he could have given me would have fixed the huge hole in my self-worth.

I knew I was broken. I knew I messed up our relationship. I caused chaos to see just how far I could push someone. I don't blame him for walking away, but I hated myself knowing I was the cause of it. I lost, and I was prepared to take down everyone around me. Kathryn was the unfortunate person in my war path the day before my first show after the breakup. I figured I'd already let go of this great guy, so why not just blow up my relationships with everyone else who loves me?

I couldn't tell you what the fight was about at that dusty country festival, but I'm sure Kathryn could. All I remember are the bitchy things I said to her, that it was the first time I saw her cry, and that she left me there. After that day, we formed an understanding. I knew I needed to stop projecting my misery and self-hate onto the people who love me. Kathryn showed me she wouldn't ever leave me, even though she ditched me at that dinky fair. If I could have, I would have left me there too.

Her love is loyal. Her love is present. Her love is godly. Her love is unbreakable. Her love is safe. I think back to all the times she has watched me not respect myself or not listen to her time and time again. She must've felt like she was pounding her head against a wall.

She saw me through every one of My Ex's affairs, from the first to the last, and everyone in between. She never left my side. She continued to speak the truth again and again until I listened to her. She knew I deserved better, and though I know every time I took back My Ex she was upset, she loved me more. She would sit there and, bless her, she would listen to me justify his actions. In those moments, she knew she could only offer me support, because no matter what she would say, I wouldn't listen or change my mind. The number of times she had to call my lawyers back and tell them I wasn't ready to divorce was one too many. She knew my bottom line, though. When I confronted My Ex the final time, Kathryn was by my side, holding me accountable and channeling strength for me. This time, I chose to believe what she told me: I could get through this.

But as I lay on the floor, with Kathryn beside me, I thought, "There's no way I can get through this. *How* the hell do you not see that I'm a complete and utter mess? I'm sprawled on the floor shaking and having a panic attack and you think I can button this up and bring my kids to school like this?"

I looked at her.

She said, "Get up, eat this protein bar, get dressed, and drive your kids to school. You can do this. You *will* do this. And then when you get home you can cry all day long until they need to be picked up again. And I will wait here for you to come back."

I hated her answer. I thought, "Right now is not a good time for tough love."

Looking back, though, I know it was exactly the right time, and what she said was exactly what I needed to hear. I had to prove to myself that I could do this and I did. I finished my protein bar because I had to. I drove my kids to school, although the seven-minute drive felt like thirty, and I muscled every bone in my body to sing along to their favorite dinosaur song on the way. I dropped Jace off first, then Jolie. At that moment as I looked back at her big brown eyes in the rear-view mirror, there was so much I wanted to say to her. I could feel the tears welling up in my eyes. I wanted to hold her. I wanted to say I was sorry for how her life was about to change. I wanted her to know how much I loved her and that I was doing this for her and Jace so they would have happy parents, not a mom and dad who hate each other and are filled with disappointment, resentment, and rage. I wanted her to know I was trying to protect her.

How am I going to tell her that her daddy isn't going to live with us anymore? How do I even start that conversation? I stopped the car at her school and I looked at her full-on, with everything I had, and said, "I love you so much, Jolie Rae." She tilted her head as if she knew exactly what I was trying to say, and she told me she loved me too. There was so much more that I wanted to say to her. There was so much more that I wanted for her and for her brother. They didn't deserve this. They shouldn't have to go through the pain of knowing separate holidays or having to stay at two different houses. I felt like I failed her. As the door shut, tears exploded from my eyes, and I could barely breathe from crying.

When I got home, I laid down on the floor of the front foyer, the entrance to our happily-ever-after home. I felt as if I didn't know which room I would feel comfortable in, so I didn't dare go any further into the house. Overwhelmingly numb, I lay on the foyer rug for hours just staring at the ceiling. Above me was the chandelier My Ex and I picked out at our design meeting when we built our dream house and the cross that we nailed up above our front door to bless our home. Again, it felt like there had been a death, and then it hit me. That's when I realized that it wasn't just my marriage that had died, but a part of me died too.

*   *   *

One of the reasons I stayed with My Ex for so long is because I was afraid to be alone. I had terrible anxiety that often woke me up at three o'clock in the morning and sent me looking for safety (more on that later). If I was going to be alone at night, I would be in a panic all day. Like my character Alex Dupre on *One Tree Hill* said, "I hate myself when it's quiet." I never related more to a character than in that scene.

Yet here I was. Alone in this house, alone with my thoughts. Alone, alone, alone.

It was so quiet I could hear the hum of the cold air moving through the air-conditioning vents into the house.

I waited for the anxiety, that rush of nervous energy, to run through my veins. Where was it?

A thought came to me: "Hadn't I always been alone with My Ex?" As I lay on the rug, feeling almost too heavy to get up, the Nashville sun pouring hot white light through the windows framing the front door, I realized I had been more alone these past six years than not.

*   *   *

Recently, I had a guest on my podcast, *Whined Down,* who said, "The cracks in the foundation are caused by the root." He meant that quite literally, that tree roots pushing into the concrete can cause it to crack. You can treat the cracks in any way you want, but if you don't get rid of the roots, they will always come back.

Until you find out where the roots of your issues lie and deal with them, the foundation of who you are, your self-esteem, will just keep cracking. What is the core memory or incident that has caused the cracks in your foundation—and why? What will you do with the knowledge once you know? I know I want to be someone my kids look up to. I want them to fight for themselves. I want them to know it's okay to feel broken or defeated at times, but that no one will ever be able to clip their wings to fly. Let me be the first to tell you, there is beauty to be found in what is broken. But it is impossible to find that beauty when we are zombies walking around in a ghost house of almost happily ever after.

How do you find beauty in the worst of times? Jesus was rejected more than any of us. He knows what it feels like to be betrayed by the ones you love, which is why "the Lord is close to the brokenhearted and saves those who are crushed in spirit" (Psalms 34:18).

Enduring a broken heart will make you feel lonely and question your worth, but God is always there to see you through. I've noticed God finds a way into my life during periods when I've experienced rejection. It's during these times that I most feel his presence, so if you are going through something difficult, trust that he is going to bless you and show you the path he has planned for you. There is such beauty in leaning into your faith and feeling someone's love, a love that has never left or abandoned you. God will not leave you; he will not forsake you even when you yell at him or leave him. He will show up for you. I have seen him show up for me in my darkest moments. It's so hard to feel that love when we can't touch it physically, and especially when we can't visualize it in our moments of pain. That is where I learned the lesson of looking up, not down.

The common thinking when going through a hard time is to keep your head down and power through it. I don't know about you, but I have spent too many seasons of my life looking down and keeping my frame of reference narrow simply for the sake of putting one foot in front of the other. Progress is always better than standing still, but I was missing something when I kept on for the sake of keeping on.

Instead, I say, "Look up, God is trying to show you something." I want to look up. I want to see all the possibilities in front of me. Yes, this might mean that sometimes I am available for all the pain and suffering happening in my life, but I also see the sunsets, the smiles, and the many paths and opportunities before me. I do not want to spend another moment powering through a painful situation that isn't right for me, and I know now that God does not want that for me either.

This first month after my divorce, I would say to God every morning, "Show me the beauty." Some days that beauty is as simple as a kiss from my kids or laughter with friends. Recently, when my heart was feeling sad and, honestly, a little lonely, God blessed me with the best sunset I've ever seen in the Nashville skies, reminding me at that moment that I'm never alone. If I had been looking down, I would have missed beauty in what God was trying to show me. If I look down, I will miss the smile I get from someone walking on the street, or the look on my kids' faces as they run through the sprinklers. Keeping my head up with intention and finding beauty in the world around me became almost like my daily reminder to stay positive.

• • •

After filing for divorce, I became hyper aware of all the work I needed to do on myself. The foundation of my life wasn't cracking, it was cratering. For so long, I thought the cracks were caused by My Ex. I wish I could say I kicked him out with confidence and never turned back. But the cracks weren't only in our relationship—they were in me. I had problems in terms of my self-esteem. I viewed myself on a low level and treated and spoke to myself accordingly. What I said and what I did weren't aligned. I'd want things but settle for other things instead. It was time to stop pouring concrete over cracks and dig myself up at the root.

Digging myself up is the only way to describe the next few weeks of my life. After my day in the foyer, I found a way to be at my kids' school at pick-up time, make them food and put them to bed. I found a way to do it the next day too. Friends came over the first weekend after he'd left, and we boxed up My Ex's things. I took breaks to "pee," but I was just taking a break from everything, staring at the walls of the bathroom, willing myself to look up, to experience the feelings, even though they hurt. I would emerge to find everyone giggling and duct-taping boxes shut.

The Next Chapter

Word to the wise: breakups are better in the summertime. Feeling the warm May sun on my skin helped. The good weather made things better for Jolie and Jace too. We would wake up in the morning and eat cereal outside on the patio. We changed into our swimsuits before the sun came up and were by the pool all day. The neighborhood kids, towels wrapped around them and their wet feet tracking water on the floor, ran in and out of the house all day, especially for snacks of cut apples and string cheese. The long days were bright and full, and the sun kept my wandering mind baked in its heat. The days slipped by, one after the other.

One day My Ex came over to pick up some more of his stuff. We hadn't been talking face to face. My lawyer was in communication with his, and the lack of control of what was going on had me spinning inside. I didn't even know where My Ex was staying. I knew he was trying to find a place to live. During that time he asked to put the kids to bed a few nights; when he came over, I would just bite my lip. I hoped he would simply disappear from our lives forever. Then again, was that something I really wanted?

Suddenly, seeing him, I felt present in the reality of our situation. The divorce was happening, and the longer we both waited to finalize it, the harder it would be to move on.

The divorce itself and all my legal conversations and questions ate me alive at night. I was told not to communicate with My Ex about the logistics, but how could I not say anything? This was my life. This was my money, money that I had fought to earn for years. I was the girl who stole toilet paper from the Wood Ranch BBQ & Grill and ate frozen taquitos

36

for a grueling year while I tried to make it in LA. I was broke for most of my twenties and in the red, accumulating debt. Somehow though I always managed to get out of the red. Work on *Grey's Anatomy*, *Entourage*, and *Friday Night Lights* would get me out of the red just enough to take a breath for a month.

It wasn't until I booked *One Tree Hill* that I was able to keep money in the bank. Looking back, it wasn't a lot of money, but I felt I had made it, hit the jackpot. I remember the first time I bought something expensive: a three-hundred-dollar ring, portraying a bird that had opened the cage, and I remember staring at it thinking, "This is me. A bird out of her cage after all these years." I was with Sophia Bush, who kept telling me to buy it, that I could afford it because I was a series regular now. The price tag made me choke, though, and I kept saying I couldn't afford it. In the end, I bought the ring. I was sick about spending that money for more than a week. Then one day, I looked down at the bird fleeing her cage on my hand and knew she found a home.

In the entertainment world there is no promised tomorrow. I could have a job today and be without it before I even know why. I've always been aware of this; since *One Tree Hill*, I have hustled to get work; I never want to be in the red again. I'm also very careful with money because I didn't grow up with it. I worked from an early age. My mom was a single parent who worked three jobs, so if I really wanted something, I had to work for it.

With the divorce, I was afraid of being put in a situation where I could lose everything I had worked for. It was complete

37

torture. As I watched My Ex pack up his whiskey bottles, so many questions ran through my mind. How much is he going to ask for? Is he going to fight the postnup? What has he said to his lawyer?

I should have stayed quiet, left it to the lawyers to handle, but in my true fashion I asked, "The money. How much do you want?"

"I have a number in mind," he said.

I replied, "Okay, so tell me."

"We should let the lawyers deal with this."

Point to My Ex. He was right, "We should let the lawyers deal with this"—but guess what? I didn't want the lawyers to handle everything because I couldn't handle the stress and anxiety of constantly worrying and losing sleep over what I would have left for money while everything got worked out in the discovery process in court. That could take a year—or more—and that meant I'd have to spend more money in lawyer's fees. My Ex was also spending thousands of dollars on our credit cards on guns and golf clubs, and I needed all of that to stop. I needed us to be separate for good. I needed to eliminate all that stress.

That's why I thought I should spend more and give My Ex what he wanted. At the end of the day, my peace of mind was worth millions, (well not *millions,* but you know what I mean), and something told me that despite my scarcity mind-set, I should have faith that everything would come back to me this time in beauty, not ashes.

"Tell me what you want," I said.

"Half."

I choked. I actually was at a loss for words and spun around to him like he was the devil incarnate.

"You want half?" I said repeatedly. I couldn't believe it. He thought he was entitled to *half.* Then I said, "So, you're fighting the postnup?"

"Yes. You forced me to sign it anyway."

"I didn't make you sign anything," I said. "You knew what happened if you cheated again."

Obviously, he didn't care. Now that I knew his plan, I had to strategize one of my own.

After he left that night, I created my first-ever Excel spreadsheet. I made three columns. The first column, Some, showed what My Ex would get in the settlement if the judge honored the postnup that he signed after he was caught cheating for the first time. The second column, Half, showed how things looked if we split things equally and fairly. Then there was the third column, Everything, where he got every commercial project we had done together—every Instagram ad, every podcast episode ad, every penny of the advance for our book and then some.

I called him later that night to see if he wanted to review our options together. An hour later, he rang the doorbell. We sat in the bedroom, and I watched as he looked over the spreadsheet. He put down my computer and immediately brought up childcare. I figured this was coming and I was glad he was being direct about it. This is what it was going to come down to: either getting more time with the kids or getting more money. I wanted more time with the kids, and he knew that. In the end, I agreed to give him what was spelled out in the Everything column, and I walked away with more time with the kids.

We shook hands, and I called my lawyer the next morning. I told my lawyers what My Ex and I had agreed to, and asked them to draw up the papers for us to sign. I guess I might have won a better settlement and paid him less if we had gone to court, but he could have won, and then I would've walked out feeling like the girl at the Wood Ranch again. I didn't play out those scenarios in my head, though, because I didn't want to dwell on the what-ifs. I needed to be done, to start fresh. I had to believe that I made the right decision of not going to mediation sessions and, ultimately, court. My Ex and I are both fighters, and both of us would've gone down swinging, but that night we acted like adults and did what was best for the family.

As he was leaving, My Ex said, "You know, I never *really* loved you."

He wanted to hurt me, and news flash, it did. I had taken massive steps away from him and toward a new future in the last few weeks, but hearing those words confirmed the little voice in my head that had been telling me that everything he did and said in our marriage was because he didn't love me. That I had made it all up, that our marriage was just a great lie. I felt deep sadness for what we both had lost.

So yeah, some low-ball, clichéd insult did hurt me, but I now know it wasn't about me at all. He only could love me the best way he knew how. The real issue was that he didn't love *himself*. Learn from my experience: People often say things out of their own hurt and anger, so any time someone tries to throw something at you, don't put it on. It's not yours.

40

. . . .

A few weeks later, My Ex took the kids on a week-long vacation. This was the first time I'd been away from them for more than a week and the first time we weren't vacationing together as a family. I didn't like the idea of them making family memories without me. I wanted to be there with them. I'm their mother, I'm supposed to be with them.

We had planned this vacation with his family pre-COVID, but when COVID hit, we had to cancel it. I remember helping to pick out an adorable beachfront property in Florida where I imagined we would all play on the sand, eat loads of ice cream, and drink wine at night.

The day the kids were leaving, my calendar alert for "family vacation" went off to make things worse. I just hadn't deleted it.

When My Ex pulled up in the driveway, I hugged my kids as tight as I could. The excitement in their eyes was the only thing holding me back from crying. I kissed Jace and Jolie goodbye, and then they were gone. I shut the front door and sat down on the floor in the foyer, once again the only room where it made sense to be. I think I might have sat there crying for four hours. What was I going to do with myself? My friends were texting and calling, all I wanted to do was go to bed and not wake up until the day they were coming home.

I got into bed, pulled the covers over my head, and let the phone ring.

I started to countdown the days. Day One, when one of my best friends, Sara Brice, showed up to check on me, I tried to play off my silence casually, and said, "Oh, you were trying to get a hold of me?" When I shell up and get quiet, friends like Sara Brice know that's when I need them the most. We sat in bed and watched *Waiting to Exhale*, and I cried and laughed and cried again.

On Days Two through Four, I used Mel Robbins's 5 Second Rule to help me to get up. You count down from five and by the count of one, you're supposed to start to kick into action on whatever you've been thinking about—for me, obviously, that meant getting out of bed. It worked. At the count of one, I would head to the kitchen or go outside to sit in the sun or take a dip in the pool. On Day Four, the silence almost felt okay, like a sign of something I might start to like at times.

Then there was Day Five. I rarely open Facebook, but on Day Five, I did. There they were, my kids, My Ex, and My Ex's family, enjoying gelato on the beach. Gutted, I got back in bed and pulled the covers over my head.

Day Six I wallowed in my sadness and drank wine. On Day Seven when Jolie and Jace came running in, little faces kissed by the sun, it was almost as if no time had passed at all. Another silent moment of going, "I didn't die, I was okay, but it wasn't easy." I started thinking that maybe I could have done things that were good for me like reading a book, enjoying the quiet, or hanging out with a friend. This go-around I chose the other path of self-pity and grief, but that's not to say I might have learned a lesson. Maybe next time, I'll take a trip or fill my time with things that would bring me joy even in the pain of being without my children. That's easier to say in hindsight, but I did learn that wallowing wasn't as fun as reading a new book or going on an adventure might have been. Being without my kids was never going to be something I would actually choose, but at least I had ideas of things to do next time. At the end of the day, if my kids are happy, I should be too.

During that week, I found that I was alone with a new version of myself. There was an old part of myself that I had abandoned many years ago. This might be a fresh start, a chance to do things differently for her. After going down the same path time and time again, this was an opportunity to make different choices than I had before. Taking a new way can be terrifying because it's an uncharted path. It looks and flows differently, and it requires a braver, more flexible version of myself to walk through it. If you're like me, you can be stubborn and set in your ways; you try to always make do with the path you're walking, even if it is uneven and overgrown. But is that way of thinking working for you? I kept tripping on rocks and becoming entangled in brush repeatedly on the path I followed.

When you hit rock bottom, you will re-emerge and choose a new path, a way of living that is true to who you really are.

When I was at my lowest early on in the divorce I had a friend who laid with me in bed as I cried and repeated the words, "I'm going to be alone forever," and she tried to talk truth to me but I didn't listen. I didn't believe her. She was happily married so what did she know? "She will never have to deal with this," I thought. A year later I found myself sitting with her as she wailed in her car after signing her own divorce papers. I was able to be there for her.

This experience has truly shown me just how God works

43

and what he does with time and how he works through others. It's so hard to see or feel you will ever be happy again when you're in it, but what I kept telling my friend was that she gets to choose her path how she wants it now. She gets to call the shots, and she will be happy again one day and she will get through this, just as she told me a year prior.

Her response, "My life will never be the same, and he robbed me of my happily ever after."

She was right.

Your life may never be the same, but it can be even more beautiful than the life you had. I wanted my marriage to work and my family to stay intact, but it didn't. I went through all the emotions on that end, but I realized sitting in that misery and resentment did no good. I couldn't change the course of things. What's done is done. But what isn't done is mine—and yours—to choose and create anew. You get to create your own life story.

So much redemption comes from lifting ourselves up from our lowest point. On any new path, you'll encounter obstacles that can potentially reroute you, but who you are becoming, who you want to be, and what you want to see will keep you on the right road. I've been detoured onto darker roads a time or two, and I had to keep reminding myself of what I truly want in my life. I want what I pray for, and I know I am going to be the one to get me there.

All love begins with choosing to love yourself first. It's about recognizing that you need to heal and grow and learn. You need to be able to look in the mirror and say, "Hey, this is hard, and I have some work to do, but I'm proud of you."

I know I have the ability to love and hope to give that love to someone, but I also know I fall short sometimes in terms of doubting my own worth or seeing red flags as carnival flags instead of what they really are—warnings. Traveling on a new path is about focusing on your healing while being aware of the cracks in the road.

When the day doesn't go as planned or the path veers, I ask God, "What do you want me to see?" or "What is the lesson in this?" In my experience, to have a breakthrough, you must have a breakdown first. Now my life, with its ups and downs, is turning out more satisfying than I could have ever imagined. The rewarding thing is that I get a chance to continue to show up and be hopeful for the new seasons. If you embrace hitting bottom and finding a new path, the light that will emerge around you and inside of you even in your darkest hours eventually will turn into the most beautiful years of your life.

Anxious

Unthinkable great things can happen, even late in the game.

—FRANCES MAYES, *Under the Tuscan Sun*

July

I knew the call was coming. I was clutching my phone on the small patio outside the apartment the kids and I were staying in while I was on set in Connecticut. Jolie and Jace were inside putting a jigsaw puzzle together. I had a puzzle of my own to deal with, and this call was the final piece.

It was three p.m. I had to be on set in an hour for a night shoot. I should have been getting ready, but I didn't want to miss this moment. Everything I had done over the last few months was preparing me for today. Signing the physical divorce papers, seeing his name—the name of the man I once called my husband—scribbled on a piece of paper and then mine right next to his. Signing the child custody document. That was the hardest to sign of all of them. It gutted me seeing my children's sweet precious names on a piece of paper that showed split holidays and time away from me. I had to pull over on the side of the road driving home after signing because the tears wouldn't stop falling. When I signed the dissolution papers, I knew there was only one last step: the official call that we are divorced. I wanted to be present when the call came in, to feel the weight of what was about to transpire. I hadn't planned on the strength of the afternoon sun, though. It was shooting down bullets of heat, and the metal strips on my phone scorched my hand. I hadn't brought sunglasses out with me either. This entire ordeal felt suddenly oppressive.

Finally, my phone buzzed. I swiped to answer it

After the usual hellos, my lawyer said, "You're divorced."

After an awkward silence, he added with a grunt and a laugh, "Congratulations."

We hung up and I sat with myself, trying to understand what I was feeling. The papers were signed, My Ex had signed them. The judge had approved everything. The seven-year saga of my marriage was finished.

I thought that this moment would be one of utter sadness or utter triumph. Instead, I felt queasy. Uneasy. There had been an almost mocking tone to the phone call from the lawyer. Not intentionally, of course. Divorce lawyers deal with divorces all day long; their patience for the sanctimony of marriage had probably expired in the nineties. Whatever peaceful "it's over" vibes I anticipated had been replaced with nausea.

I felt two forces collide. The falseness of my past relationship, full of smoke and mirrors, where nothing was as it seemed, where we talked a big game, but couldn't put our actions to our words. And this, my future. One giant blank slate.

At least when I was married, I had something to work on every day. I could grow, even if I was the only one consistently doing the work alone. Now I was *actually* alone.

Tears came to my eyes, but they weren't just out of sadness about the end of the marriage. I realized I felt uncomfortable and embarrassed. My lawyer's last little congratulations had uncovered something in me, a rotting part of my heart that I didn't want to hold on to anymore: the humiliation of treating the marriage so preciously and with so much reverence, only to have it reduced to a piece of paper for a judge to stamp. I wanted to scream, "But I tried. I really, really tried. Marriage matters to me, our vows mattered to me." There was no point in screaming, so I cried. I let the tears fall, then gathered myself, put my phone in the pocket of my jean shorts, and went back inside.

An hour later, as I walked onto set, Maria Menounos grabbed me and gave me a big hug. She knew what had just happened since the news was everywhere online, another chance for me to relive public humiliation. I was suddenly grateful to have so many people around. That night, the entire crew took a break from shooting when the sun started to go down, watching the entire sky break open into a kaleidoscope of color. We all stood there, amazed. Someone threw an arm around me, and I let myself believe it was all going to be okay.

• • •

Back in 2004, when I was nineteen, I was hospitalized in Bucharest, Romania. Alone, I lay in bed in a six-by-six-foot room at the end of a long, dark hallway with flickering lights. The hospital halls were spooky; they smelled musky and were filled with cigarette smoke. There were injured people waiting for treatment packed into small unkept rooms. I had just gotten my first break as an actress with a lead role in a movie called *Return of the Living Dead: Necropolis*. The irony of this new role and my current circumstances were not lost on me.

But this day, I wasn't filming. I had just had emergency surgery, as I was having shooting pains in my abdomen. The doctors, who spoke no English, had the translator tell me that I had to get my appendix removed and that I'd need to stay in the hospital for three days. By the fifth day of my stay, though, I wasn't getting any better. There wasn't an answer as to *why* I wasn't recovering, and they were running out of places to inject a needle to give me medicine. I had been poked so many times that the blood vessels in my arms were popping. At one point, they had to use my foot to find a vein. I looked like someone had beat me; the bruises all over my body would have proven my case to any juror.

One night, while fighting pneumonia due to my severely weakened and deteriorating immune system, I was having a hard time breathing and needed help. There wasn't a call button on the bed, so instead I just whispered a small "Hello?" There was no reply. I hobbled out of bed and peered out the window in the door of my room to the long dark hallway. I remember thinking I was truly in my own horror film and wondered why the cameras weren't rolling.

I walked down the hallway from my room. As I got closer to the main hallway, I felt waves of fear and sadness and, for the first moment in my life, anxiety. I had a knot in my stomach that would suddenly shoot up into my throat, making me feel as I were being strangled. I felt nauseous, uneasy, and faint. I couldn't find anyone to help me, so I went back to my bed and stayed up all night out of fear. The waves of anxiety came on one after the other as well as the recurring sensation that I wasn't just alone, I was *alone*. I felt so small, sure that no one would be able to reach or help me. I would have done anything to see a familiar face, to have someone beside me to reassure me that things would be okay. I didn't want to die in this hospital, and for the first time, I became unsettled by myself. I wanted—no, I *needed*—another person.

The next morning, I was told I needed a blood transfusion. I asked to call my mother immediately; given my weakened state, I couldn't imagine I would make it through the procedure alive. My mother flew in the next morning and refused to let the doctors perform the transfusion. I told my mom I just wanted to go home. Despite how I looked, she signed a hospital release. Both the smaller print on the form and the doctors warned that in my condition, I was at an extremely high risk for blood clots and, consequently, a high chance of death if I didn't keep my legs elevated. As I've said, my mother was

51

a single mom. She had three jobs and not much money, and neither did I, as I was making my first movie ever. Without hesitation, though, my mom dropped six thousand dollars on first-class tickets back to the United States so I could fly with enough room to put my legs up. When I got through customs, my dad had an ambulance waiting outside the airport. After that, everything was a blur.

What we found out was that my gallbladder was the problem, not my appendix. The shooting pains I had in Romania were gallstones. I needed to have my gallbladder removed in the next twenty-four hours as my spleen was about to burst. If that happened, I would die.

I had the surgery, and once I recovered, I flew back to Romania to film the rest of the movie, which had been recast due to my surgeries. All I needed to do was a death scene where my character gets shot to death by a zombie with a machine gun. I couldn't make that up if I tried.

Upon arriving on set, I instantly experienced my first true panic attack. My breathing became shallow, and I kept trying to catch my breath. I began to feel faint until finally, I passed out.

• • •

Fifteen-plus years later, I was on tour, playing a country festival in Mexico. While there, I had so much anxiety that I passed out and hit my head on the tile floor of the bathroom. The scar tissue remains as a bump over my left eyebrow, a friendly reminder of the anxious human I had been. That anxiety would carry through the next decade-plus of my life. Every morning at three o'clock—even when I was alone—I would wake up because my body was preparing to fight, to alert me to the fact that I wasn't safe. I didn't feel safe. *Who could come help me?*

You want to know the most insane thing that ever happened to me post-divorce? That July, I was left to figure out a new normal for myself when I spent my first night sleeping alone. All my friends had gone back to their families; their shifts of staying at the house to keep me company were over. It was time for me to put on my big girl pants and sleep alone in my house with my babies. I needed to be the strong momma they needed.

I was ready for my usual three a.m. anxiety to hit, but it never came. I slept like a baby. I didn't wake up once that night, the next night, or the one after that. In fact, I haven't woken up at three a.m. since filing for divorce.

I guess I finally feel safe.

53

• • • •

I remember the first time my father scared me: I was six years old and standing at the top of the stairs in our house. He had this look in his eyes that terrified every cell in my body. I was also six when I first saw an object being thrown, during an argument between my parents. The fight started at the dinner table one night when we were eating spaghetti. I remember the yelling and screaming. I remember wondering what would happen next, then looking across the table at my brother to check his reaction, and he looked as scared as I was. My mom continued yelling at my dad, and my dad continued yelling at my mom—and then came the flying spaghetti. They picked up the spaghetti from their plates and started hurling it at each other. When I left home twelve years later at eighteen, there were still red stains on the white curtains that hung in that dining room.

From when I was six to thirteen years old, there was always tension in my house. I remember my dad's scary stare and my mom either yelling or crying. I vividly remember always feeling on edge at home. With all the therapy I've done now around my childhood wounds, all I've wanted to do is go back and hug that little girl. The reality was that I grew accustomed to that behavior being the norm in our household. I realize now that the underlying feeling was that I wasn't safe, and that I had felt unsafe since I was six.

I have a memory of one time when my mom came into my room and cried with me while my brother got the brunt of my dad's anger. As a kid I felt bad for my brother because he always got the harsher punishment. She didn't tell my dad to stop, maybe out of her own fear; instead, she cried alongside me, and we stayed hunkered down in my room until it was over. What I learned that day was not to leave, but to stay. That moment will come full circle in a way I never wanted it to a little later in my story.

In *The Good Fight*, I talked about the moment when I found out my dad was cheating. I was thirteen years old, and nothing could fool a know-it-all teenager. For a year, my mom tried to repair the marriage, but it was just more yelling and crying, and I just wanted it to stop. My mom eventually came to terms with the fact that my dad was never going to love her the way she wanted, so she filed divorce papers and my dad left the house.

After my dad left, I barely saw him. He started a family with the woman he cheated on my mom with, and though he tried to mend our relationship for years, I put up a stone wall and tolerated him at best. I felt abandoned, and that he ruined our family. It wasn't until I had years of all that lovely therapy and living through everything with My Ex that I could find forgiveness for my dad too. I believe people can change, but more important, I found empathy for a man who never looked at how his childhood wounds played a part in the despair he created in his relationship with my mom. Today, there is peace and love for him in the family. He's become a present and loving grandpa, and that's all that matters to me now. I may not have had the model of an emotionally healthy father in my childhood, but as an adult I have witnessed his change and grace.

My dad leaving was the start of my issues with anxiety. I started to think that if I had been better, smarter, prettier, worthier, my dad wouldn't have left us . . . right? Like a million other girls whose parents get divorced, I put my self-esteem and hopes for the future in the hands of my high school boyfriend. That didn't work out so well. He cheated on me after the Sadie Hawkins dance. From that day on, this experience combined with my dad leaving our family changed me. I felt with an absolute, deeply ingrained certainty that men would hurt me, betray me, and abandon me without so much as a look back in my direction. I became a version of myself that I would have to break away from years later.

I became very codependent; I became whatever men wanted me to be.

55

"You smoke cigarettes? Cool, me too." A pack a day later I was a true American Spirit yellow-pack girl.

"You don't smoke? Yeah, no, me either. That's so disgusting."

"You like me with my hair up?" My hair would be up every time he saw me.

"You don't like that friend? Yeah, you know what? Me either. I noticed she was being possessive."

"You love rock music? Me, too," I would say as I hit Shazam to see who sang the songs he likes. I would do a deep dive for the next week learning all the songs.

I thought that if I was the perfect person a guy wanted me to be, he wouldn't leave me. Of course, in doing that, I forgot who I was. I had zero self-worth. Today, I'm honest about every skeleton in my closet as well as what I like and what I don't. You either like me or you don't. I won't change who I am to fit the mold of the person I think someone wants me to be or who they want me to become.

• • •

It was during this perfect storm of dysfunction that I met my first husband. At nineteen, I was a cheery, bright-eyed girl just trying to live out my dream in LA. He was a good fifteen-plus years older than me. I met him at a Coffee Bean on Fairfax and Sunset, and his bad-boy charm made my heart race. In fact, he could charm just about anyone. He said he was a DJ for Eminem—had the DJ cases and everything. I'm not going to lie; my Detroit heart skipped a double beat for that. I didn't doubt for one second that he had met Eminem or that he was a DJ, but I didn't find out the truth about both of those things until a year or so later.

He was alluring and kind, and he made me feel like a princess. I remember riding around LA thinking, "Wow, I found it." Did I mention he had a criminal record? Yeah, I left that part out to myself for sure. In my defense I only was told half of the truth about his criminal record, but still. Look, I'm not saying anyone with a criminal record is a bad person who can't change but learning this fact didn't affect me at all—like, I didn't even blink. I just thought, "Oh my God, this amazing guy wants to choose me."

Then I did one of the most stupid things ever. After knowing each other only two weeks, we started joking around about getting married. Can anyone say red flag? Well, not me, because, again, someone chose me, wanted me.

If I was honest with myself, I wouldn't have done it, but like I said before, I wanted to be the person someone else loved. I had this huge hole in my heart; my desire to be loved overshadowed any red flag I saw.

Two weeks later, we went to Las Vegas on a romantic spur-of-the-moment trip. Little did I know I would let an Elvis impersonator marry this man and me through a drive-through window. It's true. Elvis said, "Hubba, hubba, you're married," and off we drove onto the Vegas strip. On my wedding day, I wore green Abercrombie & Fitch cargo pants and a white Von Dutch shirt—not exactly the lace princess-cut designer gown that I had imagined I'd wear someday.

As we toasted our wedding with a chocolate sundae at the

Hard Rock Café, I had a pit in my stomach, but not from the ice cream or the Shirley Temple I drank because I was underage. I started to think, "What did I just do?"

When we got back to Los Angeles, I said, "Okay, that was so funny, but we are going to annul that, right?" I mean, Britney Spears got married and annulled it, so I figured that's what I could do too. Wrong. He was so upset that I suggested annulling the marriage that he didn't speak to me for two months. I couldn't call any of his friends, because I never met any of his friends. I had no way of finding him. He literally disappeared. I had this "husband" out in the world who I couldn't contact. I couldn't confide in anyone because how in the world could I tell my friends let alone my mother what I just did?

I had booked *Return of the Living Dead: Necropolis* in Romania, so I flew to an unknown land still not knowing where my "hubba hubba husband" was. Finally, when I was in Romania, I got a text from him saying his dad had died. Hearing that, I gave him grace for the hard time he was going through and decided to put the annulment comment to the side until after I filmed the movie. His dad's death turned out to be a lie, but I didn't find that out until later.

The abuse began when he came to Romania to see me. I was feeling down about myself because I was a little heavier than I am now. Thirty-six pounds heavier, to be exact. He called me fat, which really hurt my feelings. I wanted him to comfort me, not agree with me. I started to cry and I told him that what he said hurt my feelings and the next thing I knew, he hit me and threw me into the wall. There I was, defenseless, feeling fat and unlovable, and again not good enough. The long-standing belief that I had about myself had just hit the highest peak. And as an abuser, he had me just where he wanted me. Abusers have the uncanny ability to build you up and then tear you down just as quickly. Abusers look for someone who is vulnerable. They convince you that your insecurities are warranted, but they can look past them. They start to isolate you from your friends and if you start to pull away from them, they love-bomb you to blind you from their poor actions.

Then comes the trauma bond. Trauma bonding is when a victim has learned that they need to be "good" to receive love. It often happens with neglected and abused children, as they begin to learn that love and abuse go hand in hand. In order to receive the care they need, they need to perform for it by taking care of the angry, neglectful parent or by conform-ing to their expectations. The same thing happens in intimate partner violence cases. The victim starts to learn that if they behave well enough and if they follow the rules, eventually they will get some of the love they are craving. This bond keeps the victim believing that the abuse is a signal that they will soon get some of that love.

This is a cycle that repeats itself. Every time my first abuser would hit me or say awful words, I would try so hard to please him, to earn his acknowledgment and his love, for him to tell me that I was enough. I wanted and needed to please my abuser because his love validated me. His actions and love told me I was enough. His abuse told me I was bad, and I needed to show him I wasn't.

The next year of our relationship swung from extreme highs to scary lows and back. When we were good—let me correct that—when he was nice, I was happy. But when he was in a dark place, I was terrified. His abuse was gradual and calculated. He knew how to break me and degrade me bit by bit and, in a way, I sometimes think he enjoyed it. It almost became a game to him, and I knew I wasn't the first victim.

The next year was a complete nightmare. I was thrown out of a moving car, choked in a stairwell because I bought Tylenol for a headache—he didn't think we could afford the medicine. I was locked out of our apartment. I had my head bashed into bathroom mirrors countless times and was choked and shoved on a weekly basis. Almost every morning around three o'clock, he would throw me out of bed after coming home from a rager at a club.

He threatened to ruin my career and he succeeded. Managers and agents dropped me. I started not to show up to auditions because I was bruised from the abuse the night before. The more he hit me, the more I wanted him to love me. And he often threatened to kill me. The more I tried to get his approval, the more I disappeared.

Toward the end of our, let's just call it, courtship, I was his rag doll. I was so depressed and scared, and all I wanted was an out, but I was trapped. One night I prayed to my grandpa, who had passed away and I always considered to be my angel, saying, "Grandpa, I need you to make it so bad that I have no choice but to leave." That night, at three a.m. as usual, he threw me out of bed and said he was going to get his gun to kill me. I ran out of the house and hid in the bushes, asking myself, "How in the world did I get here? How did I let it go this far?"

After twenty minutes of hiding, I saw his car leave and re-alized it was my chance to escape. I ran back inside the house to grab my keys, but I didn't know that he was pulling back up the driveway. When I ran out the front door I saw him within inches of my car. He had his hand behind his back like he was holding a gun and I thought to myself, "This is it." As he walked closer to me I started to plead with him but he threw me on the ground and started punching and choking me. He held his left hand on my temple, and that's when I saw it wasn't a gun. When my mouth was free from his hands I screamed, "Please, my mom, please stop!" At that moment I was thinking about my mom, how sad she would be that I didn't talk to her about this, that I didn't tell her what was happening. As I tried to gouge his eyes with my one free arm, I knew I couldn't fight anymore, and this two-hundred-pound man was going to win.

For a brief moment I saw it all. I saw my funeral; I saw my mom standing over my dead body, and then I passed out on the driveway from the lack of oxygen. I think he thought he killed me and left. After I woke up and the police were called, I knew I couldn't go back. My grandpa had answered my prayer; now I needed to be strong and walk away. My husband was charged with premeditated attempted murder. A few weeks later, he was found guilty and sent to jail.

•   •   •

I had experienced anxiety for most of my life, though I was never really sure of the true source: sometimes I thought it was that near-death experience in Romania; other times, I thought it was my early childhood or my first marriage, but on most days I chalked it up to my own DNA.

Jana = anxiety.

That message had been cemented into my soul by me and those around me. I felt anxious, so I acted anxious, and then I was labeled anxious. That label became a diagnostic prison that was hurled at me constantly, especially by men. I did have anxiety. But for five or six years, since I met My Ex, really, and became a mom, there had been such a regular onslaught of anxiety-inducing moments, I truly couldn't pinpoint why I was still so anxious, especially when the trauma of Romania and my first abusive relationship was so long ago.

Worrying about the kids' health and well-being was part of it. Was the temperature in their room too hot? Were they eating enough vegetables? I had in vitro fertilization for both kids that sent my hormones through weeks of hell and my anxiety to heights I didn't know were possible. Add to that the uncertainty of my career and whether I'll book an audition or not, and the pressure to continue my music career. All these stressors were things many women faced, so why was I so undone by them? Or were we all going a little nuts trying to cope with it all?

And then there was the cheating. The worry that with every lit-up screen on My Ex's phone, I would be met with the crushing reality of another infidelity, or when I did go searching that I would yet again find something. Add that on to the previous affairs, the difficult years together, and all the work I had done to stay with him and work through it all for my family—well, just typing this has made me feel anxious. The reality was that in my marriage, the discovery of each new lie, and even the potential that I might discover one, sent my body into full crisis mode. There were so many times I would scream until I would almost lose my voice when I would find out that something was going on. It was as if I was having a series of nervous breakdowns, and my body was keeping the score of every one of them. Anxious attachment is when people are nervous or stressed about their relationship. They are afraid that the other person doesn't want to be with them. The problem is, when someone is anxiously attached, their partner eventually begins to pull away to get some space from them and their constant need for reassurance.

I was so anxious to keep myself together, but really, I was the most out of control I've ever been in my life. I was trying to control a man so I wouldn't lose my family, so I wouldn't lose what I fought so hard for. Despite the true sweat and tears to save the marriage, it was like sand sifting through my hands. The more our foundation eroded, the harder I tried to keep it together. I couldn't fail again. I had already been a failure in so many prior relationships. My God, how would another failure look? There I was, breathing in the air of a man to fix and repair any scrape or burn we just endured so that we would be together, so that I wouldn't be alone. I wouldn't be reminded of every childhood message of shame, thinking that everything's my fault, that I'm not enough and that I don't deserve happiness. I would suffocate the happiness out of the air to have it. To have the acceptance and love of the man that I wanted so badly to love me back. The more we shook, the tighter I grabbed for whatever I could reach for. I couldn't fail. I couldn't lose my family, because then I really would be exactly where my nightmares took me . . . alone.

* * *

In July 2021, I finally made it to my annual checkup where my doctor asked me if I was still on my anxiety medicine. I said yes, but that some days I skipped taking it. He asked me how I felt, and I said, "Honestly, I feel great." I realized as I said it that I truly meant it. I hadn't had a panic attack since I served My Ex divorce papers.

"Well, how do you feel about going off of it?" he said.

The thought of not being on medicine for the first time in eighteen years made me happy, but of course, anxious too. My pills were my little security blankets and I thought, "I guess I could try. The worst thing that can happen is I just go back on." I decided to do it, even though this month would present some big hurdles, like flying across the country to film a new movie and coparenting for the first time. I was also beginning to feel nervous about Jolie's first year of school that would begin at the end of the summer. She was starting kindergarten, which meant she would be at school full days all week, and it was the most time I'd been apart from her.

* * *

I still get bouts of anxiety. My therapist says that's a good thing, though. I once walked in feeling defeated post-divorce, and said, "Amy, I had anxiety the other day and I'm so upset, and now I think I have to get back on my meds." She asked me what the anxiety was over, and I told her that it involved a situation with someone I was casually dating post-divorce. His tone and demeanor during a conversation caused me to be afraid and I could feel it in the shallowness of my breathing. Hearing that kind of tone again sent me right back in a time capsule to my past and all the times I felt anxiety when I was with My Ex.

Amy told me anxiety is just your body's way of telling you something isn't safe. She said that kind of anxiety is the kind she wants me to tune into, because listening to our bodies is one of the best things we can do. Your body is going to tell you if something or someone is safe or not; and when you can't listen to it, then sometimes, you are led down the wrong road. The way she was able to put a positive spin on my anxiety made me realize I was still on the right track, and it opened my eyes to how negative and toxic people can truly impact your body and well-being.

This isn't to say My Ex is "negative and toxic"—period and end of story. I have forgiveness for him, and our relationship has vastly improved, but in June 2021, he was absolutely that way *for me*. The anxiety he was causing me was entirely warranted and necessary, and my body was telling me not to be near him. I'm sure his body was telling him the same thing about me. That's also when my therapist helped me set boundaries in terms of our conversations. She said not to speak to him about anything that didn't involve the kids; nothing else needs to be discussed. My Ex and I kept things that way for some time; we both knew it was the best for both of us.

Remember anxiety is fear of tomorrow, fear of the unknown. I have always had anxious responses when I travel; it is the ultimate test for me. What has helped me is to stay as present as possible and to soothe my biggest anxiety trigger. What always calms my anxiety is the reminder that I am safe and not alone. I make sure to meet as many people as possible on the plane, in the airport, say hi, and smile because those things show me I'm not alone. If I feel unsafe, then I need to find a way to get myself safe if that anxiety comes up, but if I stay present, I'm most likely safe just where I am.

The journey with anxiety is a long one and maybe one day I'll need to go back on medicine, but these days I usually close my eyes and say, "I am safe, I am loved, and I got this." I also say it while looking in a mirror.

. . .

Life is messy and it's beautiful, so how do you work through anxiety when it comes up? You stop letting it be the lousy exboyfriend and befriend it instead. You lean into your anxiety. You ask yourself, "What am I afraid of?" For example, if I were to ask myself what I was afraid of at three a.m. when I used to wake up terrified, I would have said, "I'm afraid of being alone and vulnerable. Because I'm alone and no one is awake now, if I pass out, who will help me?" Where is the truth and the reality in that, though?

That is where you lean into faith. Do you need more than

that? You have your friends. I would ask some of my friends to leave their phones on so that I could call them if I needed to. Speak truth into your fears.

Another great coping mechanism I use when I have anxiety is an exercise that my therapist taught me. She instructed me to notice three sounds, observe three objects, and try to find a smell. Doing that helps divert your mind from the fear you're experiencing and will hopefully lower your anxiety. Another great tool is box breathing. Take in three slow, deep breaths, hold for three seconds, and then release for three seconds; repeat until your pulse and body calms down. If you want to add a little flair, I always like to say, "Breathe in peace, exhale harmony." Over my twenty-year friendship with anxiety, I've learned many amazing techniques that have helped me with it, but these are my favorites.

Therapy and doing Eye Movement Desensitization and Reprocessing (EMDR) also helped me to manage my anxiety, and at this point I'll try anything to continue living a less anxious life as I feel better as a whole when I'm not clinging on to life due to fear. I also don't poke the bear. I know I do not love big crowds, so I'm not going to stand in the middle of a mosh pit when I know doing that probably will cause me to feel trapped and have a panic attack. Instead, I usually stand towards the back of a club by an exit, to prevent feeling anxious. Because I hate to feel trapped, I won't drive during bumper-to-bumper rush hour traffic. Instead, I add ten minutes to my trips and take a joy ride on the side streets.

I often felt guilty for letting my anxiety hold me back from doing things in my life, so now I say let's be smart and not limit. This has been key. Find ways of doing things that make you less anxious. Like my therapist always says to me, "Anxiety gets to ride, it doesn't get to drive."

Another thing that helps is to surround yourself with people who speak the truth to you, instead of making you feel crazy. It is so hard for people that don't have anxiety to understand what we feel, but find a friend like Kathryn who convinces you they can turn the plane around, even though they probably can't.

I've learned that sometimes being around certain people makes the anxiety worse, or the feelings I have when I'm around that person make it worse. I formed an anxious attachment with my husband because I had been so scared of the bottom falling out of my life. But when I got divorced, I finally let go of that attachment—and my anxiety went along with it.

Be aware of those relationships that have a hold on your heart, but maybe not in a way that it is cared for. They may be making your anxiety worse. As soon as you let them go, you will be set free.

•   •   •

How did I become comfortable being alone, when I wasn't for so many years?

In June, I learned how to be my own friend. I realized that for the last fifteen years, and primarily the last six, I would internalize the negative things emotionally damaged people said to me as the truth and repeated them to myself like the worst friend. Think about all the times you have called your-self fat or ugly, thought you weren't good enough, or you simply just beat up on yourself. Now think about saying those same things to your best friend. The reality is you wouldn't, because those words are hurtful.

Those words are also not true. When you are at your bot-tom, you are going to believe the demeaning things unkind people say, so now is the time to speak the truth into yourself. Speak the words your friends say to you. Be the best friend to yourself. I wrote the truths I struggled with in Sharpie on my mirror: "I am enough. I am lovable. I am worthy." Some days I couldn't say the words to myself, and on others, I would simply pass by the mirror without looking. But they were there, and I knew they were there. Somewhere along the way, I started to believe them. For me the more I said them, the more I believed them, and the journey to loving myself was underway. It was the realization that I needed to be the one to say those truths to myself, not a man or my kids, just me. I needed to love me to believe it.

* * * *

Don't get me wrong—there were some really bad days. One day after the divorce, My Ex said, "I'm the healthiest and hap-piest I've ever been." That comment sent me spiraling. Was he *really* . . . this time? Was I the reason that he was so un-happy all along? Was I such a terrible wife that leaving me was the solution to his unhappiness?

My poor friends were so patient with me as I replayed the

details of our marriage over and over to them. I was just try-ing to make sense of it. I would go on walks with Pamelyn and go over the same things. "He says he has changed." "Now some other women are going to get the improved version." "Why does he hate me?" One day when we were out on a run, and I was going over everything again, Pamelyn sud-denly stood still.

"Stop!" she said. "You will never make sense of it because it doesn't make sense at all."

It took me almost a year to realize I will never understand his point of view. There were two very different realities: his and mine. I can try as hard as I possibly can to understand his reality, but I will never understand the full picture, nor will he ever understand mine. Which is also why I'll never get the apology that I want. Like my therapist says, "Stop going to Home Depot looking for bread. You're not going to get it."

* * *

None of the divorce process of the last month was easy, and I wouldn't wish it on my worst enemy, but I can't lie and say I didn't feel lighter, because I did.

In July My Ex came to get his stuff. My friend Kristen took his football jerseys from the wall while Pamelyn packed up his part of the closet so I wouldn't have to see any of his clothes. Piece by piece we packed seven years of memories into boxes. I separated the dishes, gave him his pots and pans, and let him take the bed we shared. I didn't want it. I didn't want anything in the house. As his moving truck pulled away, up the street came my new furniture, thanks to the sale of my diamond ring and other diamond jewelry he had bought me over the years. New chairs, new sofa, new bed, new mattress, new pictures: just like that, the old was out and the new was in.

With that change, there was an energy shift in the house. I felt it. So did my kids. Their rooms shined brighter, and so did our house. I thought I would miss My Ex next to me in bed. Instead, I started to really enjoy being alone. There was no tension at night, no wondering what he was thinking or what he was doing in the middle of the night when he would sneak away. I was able to sleep soundly. I started to feel whole, and each day started to get a little easier than the last.

My friends noticed the difference. I started to *feel* the difference. I started to find my freedom. I started to find peace in the quiet moments that I was always so scared of. I found myself in those quiet days and I started to like myself again.

Run

And I pray that you . . . may grasp how wide and long and high and deep is the love of Christ, and to know this love that surpasses knowledge—that you may be filled to the measure of all the fullness of God.

—EPHESIANS 3: 17–19

August

I hadn't been looking forward to Jolie going back to school. When my babies were with me over the summer, the only concerns we had were when to reapply sunscreen and how much watermelon was too much watermelon. The summer had brought with it a wave of good energy, and I was hopeful. But then a breeze would come through the trees, and I would wonder, "Was that a chill? Is it fall already?" Then dread would set in: soon Jolie would be going to school. To add more salt to the wound, not just school, but she would be starting kindergarten. Big girl status in elementary school and Jace would start his more structured daycare at preschool. I would be alone again, more or less.

But for now I had them with me from the moment they woke up in the morning to bedtime stories at night. There is nothing better than the wide-open dog days of summer for seeing things in new ways. I felt a rush of positivity and vowed to put this jolt of sudden optimism to good use.

* * *

It's amazing how your mind can control your body. How it can tell you to give up, and you do. How it says you can't, and you don't.

I had the realization that that's how I had been thinking and acting my whole life thanks to the brutal honesty of my newfound hobby: running.

You see, running sucks.

I never really enjoyed running. At *all*. I believe this is exactly what I said to my trainer Erin Opera when we started working together: "I hate running and I'll never do it." She would always say that running was the best way to get lean and lose the tummy fat that I would complain about after each of my kids were born or the morning after a few glasses of wine. Then I'd reply, "Well, I'm not stopping red wine, so I reject that message, and I'm sure as hell not running, so now that I think about it, the tummy fat can stay!"

Before the divorce I didn't work out a lot. I did my weekly two-a-day workout with Erin, but I wasn't that motivated to be in great shape. At one point during a Zoom workout, I went to the kitchen to make a peanut butter and jelly sandwich. Before you judge me, I will have you know that I was pregnant at the time! I had a craving and went with it. Being fit wasn't the most important thing for me; I saw running and exercise as a means to a quick calorie burn, nothing more. I always thought I was living in balance. In other words, move your body every day, and have a doughnut every once in a while. I would go on lots of walks, but I never had the motivation to take it to the next level with fitness. I certainly wasn't going to pick up running.

If I sit with that for a minute, I think my resistance to running is what fueled my anxiety. It made the weight of the affairs, the past, the arguments, and the unmet expectations weigh even heavier on my mind and body than they needed to. I mean this literally: I wasn't getting anything off my chest. I let the stress live in me like a bad roommate. I was sitting with it. All. The. Time. Looking back, I did such a disservice to myself, knowing what I know now about how good it is to move that stale negative energy out of your body. It took me too long to get there.

* * *

After my divorce was finalized, I had a sudden urge to do something I had never done before. I wanted to draw a line in the sand in some way to separate who I had been over the last thirty-five years of my life, and who I was going to be going forward. I needed a hobby. Toward the end of July, when the kids' summer schedules started to slow, I called Erin and told her my plan to run a half marathon. So by the time August rolled around I was on a mission to train for the half marathon and also, if I'm being honest, to have a killer revenge body. I wanted My Ex, my haters, and any men who might be on my horizon to look at me and think "Wow." I know that's not the best reason to get into shape, but I'm just being honest here. My Ex and I were never getting back together, and neither of us was missing the other at this point. But still, he should be missing me, right? Really, I wanted to get attention. If I looked better than ever, then it would have to be the truth—I was better than ever. With my recent breast augmentation— which, ironically, My Ex never got to touch—my body felt like a new body. Suddenly, I was working with a blank canvas; I wanted to be the best I could be.

At one point, I went to the garage where we kept the treadmill. I stood there and stared at it. An old NordicTrack, it was a gray-and-black torture machine; when it was on, it made sounds that can only be described as creaky and sketchy. Neither My Ex nor I had used it in months, and it was covered in a thin coat of dust.

I approached the machine cautiously. Was I really going to do this?

Stepping on, I started clicking buttons. When the old screen stayed dark, I thought, *"Hallelujah, it's dead!"*

Then I saw the extension cord limply hanging from the outlet. Shit—it wasn't plugged in. A part of me was really hoping I could get rid of it, like I wished I could with any bad memories from the last seven years.

With a jolt of newfound electricity, it came to life, the small, outdated screen flashing this prompt: "Walk, Jog, or Run?"

I thought to myself, *"Okay, I could do my typical walk on an incline, barely break a sweat, or I can run."* I remembered my relationship with exercise over the years. When I lived in LA, I had this pattern of, no joke, driving to the gym and sitting in my car in the parking lot as I stared at the entrance; ten minutes later, I'd think *"nah"* and then drive home. When I was single, my motivation for working out was to see a cute guy as I walked from the front desk to the locker room. In my thirties, going to the gym gave me the freedom to eat and drink whatever I pleased while still maintaining my body for my day job. My motivation now seemed to be the chance to show the world I had come out of this bad marriage better than ever—both mentally and physically.

After a few seconds of staring at the machine and contemplating just saying "nah" and bailing, I started a four-mile-an-hour walk. Legs moving, arms swinging, I hit up the speed to five-and-a-half miles per hour. Then I let go. I ran three miles that first day; when I was done, I fist-bumped myself in the air.

●   ●   ●

The thing with trauma or any kind of pain is you hold it somewhere in your body. I hold it in my chest, and it feels like a thousand bricks are stacked on top of me. For the longest time, the only thing that helped remove that weighed-down, suffocating feeling was meditation and therapy. Going to therapy became like a part-time job because it was the only way I could manage that feeling and find some relief.

But therapy has its limitations. There is only so much that therapy can give you. This is why people say it's important to be mentally strong, but physically strong too. When I started running that August, it felt differently than it did before. I liked the immediate flood of endorphins. Running made me feel strong and accomplished, and I liked who I saw in the mirror after I finished. I needed to feel like I was growing and changing, and I needed to see it too. I had to push myself to step outside the norm of my usual way of exercising. I almost had to prove to myself I could do it; that was an important piece of my healing and growth.

Running became my church. A lot of times when I am on the treadmill or doing laps in the neighborhood, I find myself talking to God, playing worship music, and just breathing in what I know to be good and real.

Sure, I have those days where I want to stop and give up, where my body is screaming at me, or my anxiety is creeping in, begging for Netflix and a glass of wine and a good cry, but that's the challenge of my mind. Running is such a mental game because our bodies can handle it, but our minds are telling us we can't. On the days I struggle, some days I push through and others, I stop. I listen to my body. I'll never forget the first day I pushed to run five miles. I wanted to stop from the second I got on, but I knew I needed to push myself. When I hit the five miles, I began to cry. Not just a single tear either. A true explosion of tears. I was shedding more than just sweat, I was releasing trauma that was stuck in me.

We all struggle in life. Sometimes doing the work is not easy, but it's all a part of healing and taking care of ourselves.

If you're not a runner or you have limitations that keep you from running, there are other things you can do. Walking and hiking are two of my favorite peaceful ways to help alleviate the weight I feel on my chest. Being outside and in nature is not only refreshing but a great way to appreciate its beauty, a beauty we often taken for granted.

You don't have to carry the weight of your troubles, trauma, or pain—and you shouldn't. By simply placing your hand on your heart, taking some deep breaths, and going for a walk, you can regain your center and release some stress. Workouts and running have shown me not only what my body can do, but what *I* can do.

I have learned that I am limitless, but I am also the one that puts limits on myself. I am the one who prevents myself from growing and healing, from being open to opportunities, from being at peace. By moving that trauma out of my body through exercise, I begin to react differently. I feel differently. My body becomes lighter, and my breathing becomes easier. When I haven't run or worked out in a few days, I start to feel that tightness in my chest again, and easily irritated, on-edge Jana comes out. That's not good for anyone—or me. That isn't who I want to be, what I want to be.

79

. . .

What might have looked like running from my past to others felt like running into my present to me. I was elated to be in this new life, in this body. But my family wasn't so sure.

Back in July, the kids and I went on our annual trip to Michigan to spend time with my family. Looking back, I was worried. The area—what I call Up North—has been my happy place since I was a little girl; it has and always will hold the best childhood memories for me. Once we had kids, My Ex and I also made beautiful memories there. The year prior to our divorce, we were packed up in an RV, playing games and laughing for hours while we drove to my family's family lake house. We spent time tubing and having fun by the campfire with the kids. We were a happy family; in fact, some of my best memories of us as a couple were there.

Before we arrived, my mom had warned everyone not to talk about the husband-size hole in the room when I walked in. No one was to ask me what happened or how I was doing. No one was to say My Ex's name or the word "divorce." She didn't want the visit to be ruined because My Ex wasn't there.

Everyone watched as I struggled at times with being a single mom caring for two kids and accepting my family's help. I could feel them close by when I would sit on the sand alone while the kids napped. I knew they wanted to ask questions. When one aunt finally asked me about the divorce after tiptoeing around it the first few days, I said, "Listen, I'm okay." Because I was. I *was* okay. I was in my happy place, and though this year was different than the previous year, I wasn't going to let My Ex ruin my favorite place in the world and the best week of every year.

I embraced quiet moments out on the lake as I sat in my kayak remembering the photo that we captured last year of us kissing under a tree. We were the happiest versions of ourselves up there and instead of missing him, I was able to find a moment of gratitude for the small moments when we did have a good time. Whatever he was doing when he was up there, whether he was being honest at that point in our relationship or not, Up North felt like a safe zone. Nothing could touch or taint that place.

I wouldn't even think about what My Ex had been lying about when we were up there. There are a lot of memories I can't look back on because I know the truth of what was going on now, but even when he was cheating and I didn't know when we were up there, it didn't matter when I reflected on those memories. We were happy as a family, and those are the memories I'll keep.

I did make one change to the July trip: one morning, I asked my mom and my aunts if they wouldn't mind watching the kids so I could run. I had started to realize how much I needed to run. How good it made me feel. How it shifted the rest of my day. I knew I could ask my family because they wanted to help. I was grateful for the thirty to forty-five minutes of listening to the trees, smelling the fresh northern air, and my feet hitting the pavement on the winding roads.

One night toward the end of the trip, as the sun was setting over the lake, I was overcome by gratitude. The kids were wet from their baths, having rinsed off the sand and muddy lake water from a day spent out on the boat and playing on the shoreline. Jolie's hair was damp and clean, and Jace was snuggled on the patio furniture.

I realized, as the sky turned every shade of pink and blue, that I had emerged somewhere entirely new, and I was so happy to be here.

My mom came to sit beside me. We had been coming to this place since I was a little girl. I remembered sitting in this same spot a decade ago, a different breakup on my mind. This time, she was taking it harder than I was.

"You can't run from this, Jana," she said, with all the best intentions. She wanted me to open up to her. I knew what she was thinking. To her and the rest of my family it probably looked like I was in some kind of denial. I was going from task to task, activity to activity each day with a huge smile on my face. I was laughing, being silly, playing endless games of cards with my cousins, making food, and sleeping in. I took my morning jaunts alone, returning without tears in my eyes, but my hair pulled back and a calm, Zen-like demeanor.

I am not sure what my family was expecting from "newly divorced Jana" after the longest relationship of her life, but this sure wasn't it.

I put my hand in hers. I knew I was exactly where I was supposed to be.

I am so glad, looking back, that I *was* running, sprinting, into my new life. For so long, I had put my own needs aside. I was always giving someone another chance or moving at their pace. Now I was moving forward, at my own pace, and I was embracing that.

Most important, my kids were okay. I have a photo from this trip that was taken by my sister-in-law. The picture hangs in my office today. It's also the screensaver on my phone and my favorite photo of my kids and me to date. We are on my mom's pontoon boat. Jace is on my lap, smiling and holding on to my arm, while Jolie is leaning into me with the biggest smile of all. My face is at peace. This wasn't a posed picture. It captured exactly where we were in our lives at that moment: a family of three, safe and happy.

• • •

Post-divorce I started to document my progress with running through my gym mirror selfies. I take those pictures not because my legs have more muscles or my stomach is more defined, it's that I feel better when I see myself in those happy, elated, exhausted moments and that's the person I want to show up as always. How quickly my reason for running turned from wanting attention from others to wanting something for myself. I'm imperfect, and I don't have the best body on the internet, but it's *my* body and I'm getting it healthier. Maybe my journey will help others to start moving, to feel lighter. For me, it's knowing that I've pushed myself to go beyond what I thought were my limitations, whether I didn't succeed at something in the past or because I was afraid to try something new. I'm proud of myself for that. In a world where so many times we not only compare ourselves to others, but talk negatively to ourselves, I've found freedom and peace in being proud of the work I have done to make myself healthier and stronger.

• • •

"Get over it, enough already."

It's a sentiment that I have heard from strangers on the internet nearly every day since my divorce. Chances are that you too have gone through something difficult, and someone has told you to "get over it" with little sympathy or understanding.

Somehow, as I had finally found a way to escape constant reminders of my failed marriage in my real life, my internet life insisted on throwing it straight into my face. Every time I went online, I saw there was photo after photo of My Ex and me, and I was tagged in them all. Everything I posted—from pictures of me with the kids to verses from the Bible—was taken as some kind of reflection on my relationship. It seemed like, despite having the best month of my life and the healthiest detachment from My Ex I had ever had, the people on the internet were more attached to us than ever.

It started to become very important for me to get clear with myself on who I, Jana, really am. I am not an internet invention, a person crafted by strangers who have never met me, know my story, or frankly, have ever tried to know my story, let alone read this book. They don't know who I, Jana, am. To the world, I'm the girl that's known for being cheated on, "a mess," a "victim," and an "oversharer." We all have labels hurled at us constantly, and they make it difficult to start new chapters in our lives. Labels we acquire from our pasts cement us into the ground; we might as well be thigh deep in the mud. There is no moving forward when everyone insists that you be who they think you are.

Here's a fundamental part of my personality: If I'm asked about something, I'm going to share. If I am curious about something, I share. If I want to learn about some part of myself, I share. I share with the hope of touching or helping at least one person with anything, from parenthood, to what keeps me up at night, to the trials and tribulations of going through a divorce. If you ask, I will share—to help at least one person not feel alone in their struggles, to help someone feel like they are not crazy, to help others understand that forgiveness can take time, to know that you can still have a trigger or a hard day, even when you think you've fully moved on. It's okay.

It was never easy to read things people would say about me based off a twisted headline. I wanted to defend myself with my intentions of why I was sharing. I couldn't DM every hater even if I wanted to, and I did DM quite a few. I wanted them to understand what my purpose of sharing something was—how it helped a girl who was struggling to leave a toxic relationship. It took me a while to stop DMing the people who would say, "OMG, she's just famous for getting cheated on," because it hurt. I wanted them to see my heart, and I eventually realized they never would see it. I never wanted the infidelity in my marriage to be a part of my story. I never wanted a divorce. But this is my story. And my hope has been and will always be to be a vessel of strength and light for others to help them know they aren't alone and that there is light and beauty on the other side of the wilderness.

Not even one season ago, I was living in chaos trying to be this perfect version of Jana for complete strangers when really all I needed to do was be myself. When I met myself, that's when I found clarity. That's when I championed myself and followed my instincts. I remember telling my therapist about a situation that came up and how I listened to my gut and what it was telling me. Then I mentioned that I was truly enjoying my time alone, and I started to cry. She knew I wasn't crying from a sad place. She knew I was proud of myself, and I was.

When I was married, I used to write things in my journal, like "If I'm not happy with my life by June, I'm going to leave." Then June would roll around, and I would say, "Okay, it's summer and we're busy, so I guess if I am not happy with my life by Thanksgiving, I am going to leave." Each time I would stay, unhappy, because I didn't believe I deserved anything more. I started to just accept that I would never be happy.

Once I was proud of myself, once I had those endorphins pinging through me and I was accomplishing new things, I realized that I didn't need to have a grand plan. I just needed to show up for myself and be present. I just needed to let go and live. The thing is, we don't need to prove anything to anyone. We know our truths deep down. Yes, even you. That's all that should matter.

I used to hound My Ex with comments like, "Can't you see how this would hurt?" "Listen to me" and "Don't you see my side of this?" I also grew up not feeling heard by people. I tended to get louder and repeat myself to be heard and known. It was hard for me to believe I was truly loved, and that I wouldn't be abandoned again, so I was always looking for proof. I wanted to be understood and known so badly. All along, though, I was always looking to the wrong person for my happiness.

If you're feeling discouraged, like your story is over, I'm here to shed a little light for you. First, happiness is a choice. You can blame your ex, your mom, your dad, or whoever you want for the parts in your story that were painful, or you can acknowledge the wrongdoing and start to pick up the pieces so that you can experience happiness today. What I have learned is that the people who hurt us were also hurt. Although that doesn't take away or diminish what they did to you, it doesn't have to take away your happiness either. I would never want to live a loveless life because love has hurt me so badly in my past. That would be so unfair to myself and my heart to not allow love in because I bled in years past.

Sometimes memories can be a great gift, they can also bring pain. I struggle with that when I replay my memories of my kids when we were a family of four, but what I hold on to is the truth that there was still joy, even though the relationship with My Ex ended painfully. Joy is an emotion that I can choose instead of deflecting to the pain. You get to choose where you want to go with your heartbreak. It's all about the rebound and what you do with it.

There is a gift in the good and bad times we experience. I would have never thought I would have said my divorce was a gift, but it was the greatest gift I've ever received because it brought me back to life, and I was able to choose a new path. I could crawl into a hole, or I could do the hard work to heal and love myself again. I could shut my heart out and be bitter, or I could put myself back out there and love again.

It's not about the rip, it's about the repair. We either repeat or we repair.

• • •

You might have been made to believe you were weak, that the words others spoke to you defined you. You might still believe some shame messages that the world told you that aren't true. You might think your story is over; you have been broken too much. Here's the beauty in changing your labels and the clarity that comes with it: You don't need a new story. Your story is being made new. Your scars are the miracle of who you are and tell a story of strength and perseverance. Your story is being made new right now.

I once watched a video on Instagram, and the man being filmed said, "Show me something that has grown into something beautiful that didn't have dirt on it." That is true. You must have dirt on you for you to grow into the person God wants you to be.

When I look in the mirror now, I'm proud of who I see.

Someone on my podcast said to me, "It's amazing to me how you just keep putting your heart back out there after the past you have had and all the heartbreak." I thought about what she said and then I said to myself, "I truly wouldn't have it any other way." Falling in love with myself post-divorce is the win of the century. That's the greatest love story of this book: I love myself with or without a man.

Since writing this book, I've fallen in love with someone new, but that was only after I fell in love with myself. That was only after I realized what, and who, I deserve. That was only after I learned boundaries and the word "no." If you want to be loved, you must love yourself first. I honestly don't even like typing those words because I remember being told that and rolling my eyes. Once you truly sit with yourself, the person who was meant to love you will love you just as much as you love yourself.

Celebrate your victories.

Celebrate how far you have come.

You are not the same person you were a year ago.

You are not the same person you were six months ago.

Everything in life is a chapter. Only God knows what the next chapter is going to be, but wherever you are at its just a season. And a beautifully unknown season and chapter is awaiting you next.

Every day you have the chance to wake up and live differently. The unknown is scary, especially if you're still questioning which route to take. Trust me, once you make that leap, you will be okay. You get to choose the path you go on. And once you choose, don't walk. Run.

part two
Fall

Pray

The one whose walk is blameless, who does what is righteous, who speaks truth from their heart; whose tongue utters no slander, who does no wrong to a neighbor, and casts no slur on others; who despises a vile person but honors those who fear the Lord; who keeps an oath even when it hurts and does not change their mind. Whoever does these things will never be shaken.

—PSALM 15: 2–5

August and September

I was running late, which was unfortunate because I did not want to be the last one walking through those doors. I whipped my car into a parking space in the lot in front of Jolie's elementary school, threw my purse over my shoulder, and practically ran to the school's gymnasium (runners gotta run!). It was parents' night and the first time I would be seeing My Ex outside of our cordial, mostly silent pick up and drop offs of the kids all summer.

I didn't know what to expect, so I figured that's where feeling nervous was coming from. This was something parents did together. Would we have separate meetings with teachers? Sit next to each other all night? Would we stand on opposite sides of the classroom?

I paused in front of the closed gymnasium doors, and quietly pulled the metal handle and slipped inside.

My Ex was the first person I saw, my eye was drawn to him like a magnet. "Dang," I thought. "He beat me." He was wearing a white hat and his white Nike shoes. It's not surprising that he caught my eye, as he's so much taller than your average human. He stood out in the hilarious sea of parents sitting awkwardly in the tiny kids-size bleachers. Our eyes met for the briefest nanosecond across the bright and vaulted room, an acknowledgment that this night would be as weird and uncomfortable as I suspected it might.

I paused at the gym's doors.

Should I go sit beside him in the bleachers? Why would I? Because we are both the parents of the kid we were here to discuss? But we weren't parenting together, so why would it matter where I sat? Shouldn't we put on a little bit of a happy show for the teachers? Is My Ex having these same thoughts? If not, then why do I care so much?

As my mind ticked through the questions of this new arrangement one by one, I resigned myself to an empty yellow plastic chair with metal legs that had been set up on the gym floor, squeezing myself between two seemingly happy couples.

I guess this would be the reality from now on—feeling out of place in these quintessential parenting moments. I would have to start cozying up to uncertainty. I would have to be okay with just not knowing.

• • •

In my first book, I wrote that I have had a strained relationship with God. However, that statement doesn't quite capture it.

For most of my early life, God was synonymous with church, and church was boring. I don't remember anything from the Catholic church my mom, brother, and I went to on Sundays except for a very high-pitched singer in the choir and the sound of the pastor's voice putting me to sleep. God was someone we visited on Christmas Eve at midnight mass, where I would fall asleep on my mom's shoulder. I guess, on reflection, God was sort of like a sound machine.

My family prayed at dinner: "God is good. God is great. Let us thank him for our food. Amen." These were just recited words. I couldn't tell you if my mom took them to heart, but it didn't seem like it. I know I sure didn't. Whoever this God person was who was responsible for dinner every night, he could have cooked a better dinner than the chicken casserole or three-meal rotation my mom would cook.

My first attempt at an honest relationship with God was in 2011, the year I moved to Nashville. I remember doing this exercise at Onsite Workshops (an experiential therapy center) where they asked us to pick a higher power. I resisted. When the therapist asked what higher power I had chosen, she questioned why I didn't pick the God I grew up with, a Christian God.

"How could I trust that God when every man in my life has hurt me, lied to me, or let me down?" I said. It was true. I realized at that moment I had a real bone to pick with this God from my childhood. I was resisting him because my track record with trusting a man wasn't good.

She told me to try to picture a God that I could pray to, an image that didn't look like any of the men in my past. In my head, I created a new image for God. He was wearing Chuck Taylors and had tattoos. He was a "cool God," for lack of a better term. Think Jason Mraz meets Travis Barker. The therapist told me that from now on, when I prayed, that's the God I would need to picture in my head.

So, I did.

Before we continue with this story, I want to clarify what I mean by "praying." When I was a kid, I prayed like this . . .

Crickets.

I didn't. Again, besides the dinner prayer, there was no "Dear God, thank you so much for anything."

That's why I make praying with my kids an everyday thing, but it's not something that is forced either. My kids fight to pray first. I often wonder how different my relationship with God would have been if I had stronger pillars of faith in my household when I was younger. I see my kids, especially Jolie, close their eyes and mean every word they say. Each dinner and at bedtime, Jolie says a different prayer as she sways her head in true appreciation. She thanks God for her toys, her friends, her family, and "everybody on Earth." Jace looks over at me when he says prayers, and I see that he wants to learn. I always say to him, "You can thank God, or just say hi, whatever you want." He always throws in a thank-you for his Marvel figurine, me and his daddy, Jolie, his doggies, and he ends with "the end." My kids know they are never alone. They have mommy downstairs and God watching over them. What I would have given to feel that peace at night when I was a child.

Now, my higher power is effectively an odd blend of a Jesus-type figure and Mother Nature. I pray every night in the moment right after I turn out the light before I fall asleep. I pray by lying there quietly, taking a moment, and looking out the window at the moonlight. I look forward to that brief peaceful prayer every day, this quiet space where I just try to feel small and known and to access the most serene and human part of myself. Praying for me is also sitting out back watching the sunset, thanking God for all the moments in my life, good and bad. For all the moments, even the hard ones I can't understand. I am far more grateful than I could've ever imagined I would be. I have been blessed with the highest highs, beautiful babies, and incredible roads. Though I've walked through harsh winters and had scary lows, I know that my God is in all of it, walking through each new season with me. Prayer for me is a thank you to God, and a reflection on roads I've walked and the roads I'm going to take.

God wants us to move forward in freedom. You are never more than a prayer away from him.

• • • •

I started going back to church when I met My Ex. We went to a nondenominational church in Nashville. They welcomed everyone, even nonbelievers who are weary but haven't committed their life to God yet. That made me feel seen, that was *definitely* me. We didn't go to church regularly, but we did form a relationship with one of the campus pastors, who, in a perfect twist of fate, loved to wear Chucks. The pastor at that church became someone I looked up to so much; he spoke truth and hope into me.

Two years later, I was back on my hands and knees to God. I found that even though I didn't consider myself a believer, in desperate moments, my mind took me straight to prayer. But I still didn't *believe* believe.

At this time, two years into our marriage, I had just found out that My Ex had cheated again and was on his way to rehab. I was beyond glad to have the help of a pastor this time around, especially someone who knew me and knew My Ex and was rooting for our love story. I needed some spiritual reassurance, so I was very happy when he texted me to ask how I was doing. I told him I was sad and that My Ex was in rehab. Not even a second later, he sent me a selfie of his shirtless body in his sauna.

I was shocked. I stared at the phone. I was at a total loss for words, or thoughts, or . . . anything. I was paralyzed. How and why is a pastor sending me a shirtless photo of himself in a sauna—and why does he think this is okay?

Then I was enraged.

Is this God? Is this spiritual reassurance? Is every man going to be this way forever?

Looking at this ridiculous photo, I vowed to be done with the church and with God. I thought to myself, *"See, Jana, you were right. God is not to be trusted, even when he shows up in the form of a Jason Mraz pastor. They are all just cheaters and liars and they are never going to be there for me."*

I realized later that I was putting God on the face of people. When I imagined God in my mind, I pictured a guy that I might see on the street. I imagined our pastor as God. I imagined my father as God. I even imagined My Ex as God. But God is just who he is: God. There is only one. And that God won't leave you. He won't lie to you. He won't forsake you.

I know this because back in May, when I was in my deepest moments of despair that first week of divorce, he was there. He didn't leave me. He gave me the strength to get up. He gave me the strength to have eyes and see the truth of my relationship and life.

• • •

Sometimes when we experience a human violation like lying and cheating, we feel we have proof to say, "See, God isn't there for me," or ask, "If God exists, why didn't he answer my prayer?" I often doubted God's presence in moments like this too. I didn't understand why he would want me to be in pain or suffer from loss of a loved one.

During your hardest trials, God is making you stronger.

How do I know? Believing in God is about trust. It reminds

me of the meme of God and a little girl holding a teddy bear. The girl is standing before God, and God is extending his arm, beckoning the little girl to give the teddy bear to him. She says, "But I love it." He replies, "Just trust me." She doesn't know that God has a giant teddy bear behind his back. Having trust in God is one of the hardest things to do, but it's also one of the most freeing things when you can put your hands up and trust that he wants you to succeed, to be happy, and to learn. He will not shame you for your missteps but guide you along better paths if you let him.

I remember my hands-up moment in church. I envied the people that could lift their hands up in worship. I went from not being able to stand up in church post-divorce to months later slowly moving my hand up from my body. One Sunday my hand was in my pocket, and the next Sunday, it was out. Eventually, I lifted it high when I heard the words, "In the name of Jesus there is healing." Hearing those words there was nothing left to do but lift my hands high because there is healing in Jesus. Only a few months earlier, I was barely able to walk into that building.

Every morning I opened my Bible, and I would say, "God, what do you want me to learn and know?"

I started to walk *with* him. To listen to *him*.

My story and your story were written long before we could have ever known. God has a divine way of turning pain into beauty. Trust his plan. It may not be what you thought your story would be . . . but he has you.

In the silence, in the darkness, that is where I found me, that is where I find God.

Where is God?

God is all around you. He's the soft pink sunset. He's the rain. He's the flower that blooms in spring. He is the creator of all the beauty. God is the warmth in your heart, and the fire in your soul. He is with you all the time. He is your greatest friend and biggest champion. He knows you are not perfect, but he loves you anyway and will continue to walk with you. When you question where is God? Ask him. And I promise you if you listen close enough you will hear him. You just need to open your eyes, lift your heart, and seek him out because he is there.

• • •

An ex-boyfriend, upon breaking up with me, said, "Call me when you heal." That has always stuck with me.

We all have our faults. We all have our pasts, and we all have our traumas.

Healing isn't a straight line. However, go to any counselor or therapist, and you will no doubt hear about the five stages of healing: Grief and denial, anger, bargaining, depression, and acceptance. I can honestly say, by the time fall rolled around in 2021, I had felt every one of these emotions, looked every stage of healing dead in the eye, and finally, accepted that my marriage was over. I have moved on, and the relationship is part of my past. Years later, I don't let it define me anymore, and it doesn't hold the weight it did when we separated. That is the joy that comes with time and healing. The thing is, you need the two of them to work hand in hand. You could have all the years behind you but if you haven't touched the healing part, your anger and sadness can still live inside you and dictate your path. You mix in the healing and the time, then the two form an understanding that the past can be just that, and you get to start anew.

But healing isn't easily compartmentalized in just these five stages. I had to accept that my marriage was over before I could heal from it.

For me, healing is a prayer. Healing is God's work, not mine. Healing happens in my soul, and it happens entirely based on intention, solitude, faith, hope, and love.

Why do we need to heal? Because the greatest gift we can give ourselves on the heels of a terrible circumstance is to move on.

We all get choices in life to decide what is going to control us and how we react to that power. Someone who was hurt badly or was in a traumatic relationship can scream from the rooftops everyday if they want to about the absolute injustice done to them. If that's where you're at, I get it. But let me ask, "how is that working out for you?" Is that the life you want to live? I'm going to venture to say no.

Healing and moving on don't mean you're brushing things aside. Picking up the pieces and moving on *is* healing. And just because there aren't any more shards of glass on the floor doesn't mean that you're completely healed or expected to be. We can't always control what happens to us, but we *always* control how we respond and react.

Healing is for *you*. It is a gift meant to allow you to live a meaningful life and not let your past hold you back.

. . . .

Post-divorce was a time of healing and battling pain. When I voiced my sadness online, I was told to move on, to stop talking about it, to stop being a victim. One DM said, "We get it, OMG shut up." When I was happy, I got "OMG she moves so fast." I felt lost. I didn't know who I was or who I was supposed to be. Every part of my being wanted to move on but when I took a step forward, I felt sad, lost, and confused. I put a filter on the images I posted, and I smiled in them in a way that wasn't the most believable. Sometimes I felt strong and empowered, then within the next hour or day, I'd feel a wave of pain and disappointment that this was going to be my story, that this is where I ended up. The outside world told me I could be happy or sad, but not both. A few months after we filed for divorce My Ex said the same thing, "You can't be both, Jana." I was fake for saying "I'm hurt" but showing the world I'm happy. Why can't I be both?

I have a tattoo of an ampersand, the typographic symbol for "and," tattooed on my arm for a reason. It's a constant reminder that we can hold space for the hurt *and* the healing. The growth *and* the pain. It's being able to say, "This hurts, and I'm going to be okay." It's acknowledging that, "this feels painful and I'm healing." I feel as though we are so often told to feel one way or another. From childhood, we're told to "Get up and stop crying" when we'd fall down. When you break up with a boyfriend you hear, "He's a dick. You're so young; there are plenty of fish in the sea. Chin up, buttercup." When you get divorced and are coparenting, your friends say, "You won't have your kids this weekend? Oh my gosh, I would love to have every weekend without my kids." What if you fell and heard, "Oh man, you just took a stumble. I'm sure that really hurt," *and* "You will be okay." Or if when you broke up with that guy someone said, "I know you really loved him and you're in pain," *and* "You are going to get through this. The right one is still out there." Regarding the divorce and coparenting, wouldn't it be nice to have your friends say, "I know it's going to be really hard to be away from your babies," *and* "The time away might be nice to recharge." I use these examples because we all go so quickly to "but," to dismiss that people can still have feelings over something that hurt them for some time. We're taught to get up, to brush it off, to put a filter on our face, and move on.

By no means am I saying it's fine to sulk forever or stay sad. What I'm saying is that there is room for both at times. It's okay; it doesn't mean you're not healing. It doesn't mean that you have gone backward in your growth. Ten years from now I might have a moment that washes over me when my kids are with their dad. Now, at this time in my life, I will have long moved on, but it's still okay that I might have a brief feeling of sadness. It doesn't mean I'm holding on to the past or that I haven't let go. It's simply giving my feelings a home for both.

We are not meant to have it all figured out. We aren't light switches. Trust me, I have prayed so many times for God to just take away my ability to miss someone or grieve someone. When I did feel stuck in the memory of missing someone, I would take out a piece of paper and write down what I really miss. I would write down what wasn't working for us and me. When I looked at what I wrote, God showed me on paper that it wasn't right AND it still doesn't make it any easier with my sadness of loss. I've been told that's getting through it. Not past it. And not even over it. To say "I'm over it" almost sounds defensive. Now, you might be feeling like you are over it and that's amazing—but are you really? Instead, try using the phrase "through it," because I would beg to differ that we are ever "over" anything.

With relationships, you mourn the life you imagined you would have with this person, and then you pick up the pieces. When your heart is on the other side of the grieving, you might have memories that wash over you, but don't beat yourself up over it. You walked through the feelings, and some things might still come up later.

You don't get over a loss, you get through it. It's not easy to accept that, and the walk to get to the other side isn't easy. It truly isn't supposed to be easy. Doing the work is hard and learning about yourself through the process is even harder. Sometimes we don't see what we don't want to see. There have been many times in my life when I didn't want to look more closely at a situation because I knew what I had to do. With My Ex, I knew that would involve me shutting the door on a man. It would involve being alone. It would mean loving myself; that aspect alone terrified the hell out of me. I would have to sit alone with myself in the quiet and in the dark. I would have to look at things that I knew would be difficult to accept. But as I said, through hard times there is healing and pain. There is growth and sadness.

When you do get down and the past creeps in, it doesn't mean that you're allowing it to take over your life. It's just the reality of where you are. It's knowing that you can feel brave and broken all at once. My therapist once said to me, "There are many ways to survive. There's survival by smoke and mirrors, by sacrifice, by stonewalling, by substitution, by surrender. We move in and out of our survival guises until we can't fool ourselves anymore. When we are finally willing to relinquish the need to live through others and acknowledge that we deserve a life of our choosing, we are ready to move on and be born again." I believe surrendering to the acceptance of where you are whether happy or sad is a step in the right direction. A step towards healing.

I am healing and growing every day. Just like you. I know that ultimately my lessons and blessings are helping me to become even more myself. I do not rush my healing because we all grow in our own time. There is no rush. There is no score. You can slow down, breathe, heal, become. It is your time *and* it's the perfect time. Know that wherever you are on your journey, you are free to feel all your feelings. Just don't stay stuck there for too long. If you practice throwing an *and* in when you feel your feelings, you are essentially being the best friend to yourself. You are allowing yourself to have the feelings *and* saying it's going to be okay. In return, you will not stay stuck in the sadness. You, in a way, are your own motivator when you hold space for both feelings.

When I got stuck in the heaviness of who I thought I was, I wrote down all the words that were playing a part of my story: "not good enough, victim, abuse, buried, shame, past, narcissism, the old story, liars and cheaters." That was my narrative. That was the story I was putting out there through my hurt. I called that chapter of my life "The Broken Bird." When I looked at my Instagram and all the quotes I posted post-divorce, I looked like a broken bird. I even had a close friend say to me, "You are not a broken bird; stop acting like one."

I came to a point where I wanted to change my narrative because I felt myself changing. I felt myself healing and growing. The new words I wanted to be a part of my story and narrative were: "free, brave, light, positive, joy, intention, laughter, and calm." That's what I started to feel and wanted to share. I didn't do it to get recognition from those on Instagram or to prove that I was finally happy, but it was because that's what I truly started to move into. And the only way I got there was when I started to give myself space for both healing and pain. I started being my most authentic self and began to shine when I could hold space for my past and the hurt. I started to love myself and heal.

Who do you want to be? What story do you want to tell? What words do you want people to see when they watch your walk? Write down all the positive words that you want to exude and then say it's okay when you do have a sad day. Hold space for the dark and the light and walk with the confidence that you are exactly where you are supposed to be. There is no guide, no straight line, no timeline to healing. There is only you and the words that you speak to yourself. Hold space for yourself. Hold space for your emotions and the fact that you might feel two very different things. You may be hurt right now, and you will be okay because you are gathering the tools to get you there.

This quote by Beau Taplin has really helped me: "Perhaps the butterfly is proof that you can go through a great deal of darkness yet still become something beautiful."

Now read that again and instead of saying yet, say *and*. You can go through a great deal of darkness *and* still become something beautiful.

• • • •

Sometimes you need to borrow faith. You might not feel strong enough to feel it, or empower it, so just ask to borrow it. Then you can wear it until it feels right to purchase it, to embody it. Having blind faith is hard when you have experienced nothing but devastation or loss, but if you borrow faith, you don't have to jump all in. You can be wary of it. You can take one step at a time with it. The thing with borrowing faith, though, is the return rate is low. You start to realize you have nothing to lose. A little more faith and a little less hopelessness feels better at the end of the day.

Chase Joy

Do you know the most surprising thing about divorce?
It doesn't actually kill you.

—FRANCES MAYES, *Under the Tuscan Sun*

October

All summer, my therapist was my safe place to heal, first every week and then every other week. She tolerated a lot of feelings from me, a lot of high highs and low lows. Overall, I was faring better than I thought I would, and I thought she would be pushing me to keep going deeper, to do the "real work." She insisted on the opposite: "Chase joy," she said. She kept saying it, and I kept rolling my eyes. She would say it again, and I would politely nod. She would say it again, and I would find a way to change the subject. She said I'd been doing the hardest three years of work in her room, and for a season she just wanted me to chase joy.

Chasing joy sounded about as cliché and dumb and impractical as it gets, like a line from a Hallmark card or the slogan for a company whose marketing team couldn't come up with anything better.

My personality is prone to dramatics. I like reality television and *Sex and the City* and, of course, I can be found filming myself for my Instagram stories. You can absolutely find me weeping at the end of a good drama and living my own romantic comedy in my brain. But when it comes to my personal life, I frequently land on the cynical side. I love the big, amazing storyline for characters in movies and even for my friends, but I'm rarely giving main-character energy in my own life. I am frugal, laugh easily, and like to stay at home. I am often suspicious of other people's intentions. Prior to the divorce, I preferred to hear my friends talk about their lives than offer details about mine, as mine seemed to be the same story again and again. I was bored of talking about it and I was the main cast playing it out. Even so, I didn't want my heart to become cynical. I didn't want to become numb to everyday experiences, but I was slowly moving in that direction.

The result of this sudden cynicism, as my therapist could tell, was a kind of defiance toward joy, especially displays of happiness. Smiling, celebrating, cheering, public displays of affection, two people rushing into love or marriage, forehead kisses, Instagram posts about vow renewals, or family time. I had lost my patience with these things, and was making it known, especially in my weekly sessions.

I think my therapist worried that on the other side of my divorce, I might sink even more into this person who thought joy was for someone else, not me. Worse, that I might start unintentionally resisting joy altogether.

In a session where she once again told me to "chase joy," I responded:

"Well, I'm going to Ireland in a few weeks."

"Ireland?" she asked, perking up.

"Yeah, Ireland, but it's for work."

I could sense her excitement. "Great! After the work is done, then you go chase joy. This is your time."

I heard her, but I didn't *hear* her. I wasn't going to look at this trip as anything other than what it was: work. I was going to fly in, film, and fly out, nothing more. As I lay in bed that night after our session, her words "this is your time" ignited something inside in me. What if this really *is* my time? And what if this really is my time to *chase joy*? But logistically, how could I? If I extended the trip a day, I would have to ask for help. My Ex and I were nowhere near coparenting goals at this point. And then there's that giant note written in Sharpie in my brain that says, "You can't do that, you have anxiety."

Still, in the morning, I asked Kathryn to see if production would let me extend the trip by one day. Because let's be honest, when in my career have I ever been asked to work in Ireland? Never. The coolest place I've ever gone for work was Wilmington, North Carolina. Ireland must be a sign from God to go chase joy after all. The trip was extended, but Kathryn's passport wasn't renewed in time, so she couldn't travel with me, therefore leaving me to either cancel or hire a tour manager to fly with me. I was so close to chasing joy that I could taste it, and canceling wasn't an option. Having a tour manager wasn't an option for me either. Nothing against my tour manager, but I'm pretty sure he wouldn't be interested in skipping down cobblestone roads with me. I had an image in my head of what I needed this trip to be.

I went on a mission to find my partner in chasing joy. I asked Pamelyn to go with me, and she said yes right away. She's the epitome of free and fun, so I knew we were going to make the very best of it, and boy, did we ever.

* * *

For so long I have felt that I don't deserve joy in my life. But why? Doesn't everyone deserve this? I think it's because growing up, there weren't a lot of purely good or happy times. My mom and I used to have this running "joke" where when we talked about family memories we would say, "That was a good memory right?" We would remember something fun and then say, "Oh wait, that was when you and Dad were fighting," and suddenly the good memory was shaded with all the difficult things we were experiencing.

As a teenager, I watched all my friends get the "typical" fun experiences that I wasn't able to have. While my friends were all off traveling on spring break and taking senior trip cruises, my parents' divorce and our financial situation meant I wasn't able to go.

In my senior year of high school, my mom realized what I was missing out on, but wasn't about to let me miss out on having a senior spring break, even if we couldn't afford the one all my friends were doing. She packed up the car and drove me and another friend who was in the same situation to Clearwater, Florida (a nineteen-hour drive!). We had so much fun. I still think back on that trip and smile. (Hey, Mom, this really *was* a good memory!) The stories, the laughs, the memories of us dancing to "The Thong Song" by Sisqo—it was the perfect spring break. It may have been different than what I had originally wanted, but my mom showed me in that trip that we can choose joy. You just have to do something about it.

* * *

Once Pamelyn and I boarded our Air Lingus flight, she pulled out a piece of paper entitled "Ireland Bucket List." "Drink a Guinness," "Eat shepherd's pie," "Skip down a cobblestone street," "See the Cliffs of Moher," and "Kiss an Irishman" were just half of the funny yet memorable moments we were about to check off. As we landed in Ireland, I felt this surge of energy and excitement I'd never felt before. I was happy. Genuinely, really, really, really happy. I was smiling—and it wasn't forced. I embraced every second of the short, seventy-two-hour trip. We had one day of travel followed by one day of work, then on the third day, I hired a car to take us to Ireland's east coast to see the Cliffs of Moher, Galway, and the most beautiful castles.

Standing on the Cliffs of Moher was a holy experience. Seeing the breathtaking views, the waves crashing into the ancient sea cliffs and the views of green mountains in the distance, I couldn't help but see God everywhere. It also wasn't lost on me that the sun was shining down on me on a day when the forecast was for rain. I have been to some scenic places, but nothing could compare to what I was seeing that day. Even though the cliffs were buzzing with tourists, I felt at peace, as if I was experiencing them alone. As I breathed the fresh sea air, a feeling of serenity washed over me. As I walked along the tiny trail on the five-mile stretch of cliffs, I took in the various stunning views, and I wasn't about to miss out on any God-made creation. At the final view I inhaled a deep breath, finally feeling acceptance of what I had left behind and where I was now.

114

It was time. It was time to leave the past spring, summer, and fall behind. It was my time now, not only to chase joy but choose it. I'm glad I didn't hold myself back from experiencing one of the most extraordinary views of my life. Looking back as I write this years later, I recognize how pivotal that moment was for me. I came back to the United States feeling lighter and with a fierce desire to see more of the world and not be captive to my anxiety, fears, or doubts. I realized there wasn't any anxiety on that trip because my mind was purely focused on joy and not fear. That trip propelled me to take chances, which ultimately helped me grow more as a person. It also helped me have a little fun.

Chasing joy propelled me into choosing joy even if things didn't work out exactly as I hoped. The next summer, I flew to a bunch of different places, exploring new cities, and I didn't once feel anxiety or fear. I took more chances to experience

life, like flying to England for a wintery Christmas vacation
for maybe another shot at love. I didn't know how that would
play out, but I chose to take the adventure. That trip was
about so much more than going to see a boy or getting over
the fear of flying alone to another country. (Though I was
so proud I didn't have an anxiety attack on hour six and divert the plane back to the States.) It was about experiencing
moments alone and truly embracing and choosing joy, even
when the reality of not having my kids for the first time on
Christmas Eve was in the back of my mind. I held the weight
of both feelings, but I focused on the freedom and on the joy.
I even find myself being more adventurous with my kids now
too, in how I parent them, in how we play. I wake up each
morning and I say to myself, "Choose joy." I don't want to
live with anger or a negative mindset, so I choose joy because
it will always lead to love in your heart. God knew my mission of chasing joy, and what I learned years after my divorce
was that I didn't think I deserved it, which is why I fought the
narrative for so long. I thought it was for others to have and
experience. That's the great lie we tell ourselves, so don't just
choose joy—chase it, and find it.

Starving

Consider it pure joy, my brothers and sisters, whenever you face trials of many kinds, because you know that the testing of your faith produces perseverance. Let perseverance finish its work so that you may be mature and complete, not lacking anything.

—JAMES 1:2–4

November

Just before I left on my trip to Ireland, two of my Nashville friends invited me to their kids' birthday party, and I had been looking forward to it from the moment I got home.

With all the treadmill sessions of the past few months, and the joy chasing of the past few days, I was also very much feeling myself. I saw progress in every selfie, every smile, every inch of my body. I would be lying if I didn't admit that the thought of whether I was ready to try again with someone hadn't started to creep in.

Seriously, I am not woo-woo, a girl who believes in spirituality manifestation. You already know I tend toward the practical. However, I honestly believe I "thought" Seth into existence. No sooner did I consider wanting to try again with a new guy, then he appeared before me.

- - -

When I walked into the kids' birthday party, I felt as if Seth had been waiting for me to show up. Wearing a tight shirt with his muscles popping out everywhere, hat on backward, and the biggest grin on his face, he was shooting hoops and jumping on giant trampolines in competition with the other dads.

My friend's husband came over to where I was standing, where I had a gift wrapped up in a big bag in one hand and my purse in the other. He gave me a hug and then looked in my eyes.

"Listen," he said, "I'm not sure if you're ready yet and it is totally okay if you aren't."

I thought to myself, "Was this really happening?" I had never been set up by a friend before. Although I had just been wondering if I was ready, I found myself less sure in the moment.

"Jana, my friend is single," he said. "He's here today if you want to, you know," he paused, "talk."

"Who is he?" I asked.

"The guy in the hat over there. Seth."

I looked at Seth with new eyes. He wasn't wearing a wedding band, which I clocked when I walked in.

"You should talk to him."

I thought about it for a second. "I'm sure he'll talk to me if he wants to. I'll be here all day," I said and smiled.

My friend laughed. "Fair enough."

I grabbed a drink and went off to play with my kids and hang out with my friends.

About an hour later, I was in the ball pit playing with Jace when I sensed someone coming up behind me.

"Hi," Seth said.

I turned around. "Hi," I said, meeting his eyes.

No introductions were necessary; we already knew each other's names thanks to our friends. We were both exhausted from running around with the kids, and we had the same glow—parents having a good day with our family and friends. What more did we need to know about each other?

Something about this felt so right. Here I was, finally feeling truly ready, and here was someone I didn't need to vet through social media or even Google—my friends knew him, loved him, and vouched for him.

He was about to say something but I interrupted him. "How do you feel about bounce houses?" I asked.

He smiled. "Right behind you," he said.

• • •

There's a moment after a breakup, a painful time in life, or an all-consuming grief when you think you are out of the woods—it maybe in a month, a year, a few years, even a decade—and you aren't. That is okay. It was okay for me, and I survived.

You might think I had it all figured out or that Seth might be "the one." Let me spoil the story for you. Despite the cutest meet-cute of my life, Seth and I weren't even close to a match made in relationship heaven. We dated for less than three months before calling it quits. I battled the same unhealthy patterns from my marriage to My Ex, patterns that I had fallen into years before that.

The hard truth was that I met Seth in a new way, and I had done a lot of healing, but I wasn't ready. I still fell into the arms of the same type of man as My Ex and the ex before him. And I was the same Jana, at least when it came to relationships: boundaryless, starved for love and attention, and desperate to give away all the love I had.

* * *

One day my therapist asked me, "Jana, what's the worst thing you can do when you're hungry?"

I said, "Go grocery shopping." I got that question right! I guess I knew all too well from experience.

I had just told her about meeting Seth and how it had raised some early red flags. That's when she gave me one of the best pieces of advice she ever has: "Don't go to the grocery store when you're starving." She went on to say that when you go to the grocery store hungry, you end up picking out things that aren't necessarily good for you. But you're so hungry, you *need* to eat, so you grab that bag of chips because they are right in front of your face. That's the same thing with a relationship. When you are absolutely starving to be loved, you are going to pick the wrong person because you are so desperate for a quick feeling and quick fix, to fulfill what you want and are missing in your life, you'll take whatever looks good to you.

I didn't realize I was starving when I met Seth. I thought I was at this highest high of self-realization. But this had been a pattern in my life, and I wish I had seen it then: I'd do mountains of self-work to change and grow as a person, only to choose the wrong guy in the final hour. I would give all my newfound goodness away to the first guy that met my loosely held "criteria," and he always seemed to be the wrong guy.

Of course, there is a disclaimer to that statement. No person is inherently "wrong." Seth is the right man for another woman. My barometer when it came to choosing men was so off, I began to wonder if these patterns went deeper than feeling starved for love or being hungry at the grocery store. I am glad I can say this out loud today; it wasn't an easy thing to accept during the time when Seth and I fell in and out of love. But the truth was (and is): I was choosing men as a deliberate form of self-sabotage.

Here's how the self-sabotage pattern often played out. I would recover from a relationship long enough to get to the top of my personal mountain—feeling good, moving on— before a kind of discomfort would settle in. I would start to feel increasingly restless and agitated. My heart would become more demanding, repeatedly asking: "Okay . . . I made it . . . What *now?*" Peace was not peaceful for me. My brain and body only knew trauma and a problem to solve, and a mess to clean. And then the thoughts would come in: *"Maybe I am ready for someone new." "Maybe I should start dating." "Why not?"* Suddenly I'd end up in the arms of the first guy I had a connection with. But did I really *want* the guy? Or did I *need* the cycle of love, war, breakup, and breakthrough?

I don't mean to downplay what it means to feel ready and excited to date again, but if you've found yourself in a similar cycle, it is so critical to know the you that is showing up to try something new. Are you prone to impulsive decision making? Have you *truly* given yourself enough time to feel triumphant, relaxed, and okay? Or are you, like I was, rushing through the good part?

• • •

Only a few weeks into my relationship with Seth, I knew something wasn't right. He was handsome, charming, and his smile made me melt. But there was also something that I couldn't quite put my finger on. He seemed like he was hiding something and painting a different version of himself to me than who he really was. Still, I couldn't shake how I felt the day I met him. I mean, we met at a kid's birthday party. It was the most serendipitous moment I've ever had. We met the way you are supposed to meet someone—through mutual friends. Here it was: meeting the guy when I least expected it. When we were at the bounce house, I thought to myself, *"Wait. Is this really happening?"*

We exchanged numbers, and within a week, he had come over almost every night and spent countless hours on the phone. After eleven days, he told me he loved me. On Day Twelve, he texted, "Are we soul mates?"

It felt really good. Yes, it was crazy how fast we were moving, but I barely noticed the timing amid all the excitement, and I sure didn't care what anyone else had to say about it! Until that point in my life, I hadn't had someone touch me in the way he did. He was passionate and sweet, and being noticed and understood by him felt like a puzzle piece fitting into place. He left me notes around the house. He supported my dreams when I voiced them. He listened when I spoke and offered advice that showed he was mature, evolved, and compassionate.

"Here it is!" I thought. It had been a little more than six months since my divorce and a million years since I felt loved, appreciated, and cherished by a man. I fell into the pool of Seth so fast and was happy to drown there. I had forgotten the goose bumps, laughter, and sweet feeling of being smitten with someone.

It felt almost too good to be true, and, like most things, it was.

If I had been practicing the self-awareness my therapist had been pounding into my brain over the last six months, I would have realized I was just repeating the same pattern I followed when I met My Ex. But I was *starving*; I was not looking at the red flags because I couldn't stand knowing they were there.

Because we were both divorced, Seth and I had common

123

ground, but also a lot to unpack about each other's pasts. I remember texting him one day, asking if he cheated on his wife. It was important for me to know for obvious reasons. I am not a believer in "once a cheater, always a cheater" or that someone who has never cheated wouldn't be capable of cheating. I told him in the text that I would never ever judge someone, but that I just needed the truth. A willingness to be honest was a trait I was most definitely seeking from all future partners. On this point, I was maturing and had grown. I asked about the red flags, even if I ignored the answers.

Lying in a relationship is worse than anything else. I told him that I have done things in my past that I'm not proud of, so I wouldn't judge him at all. I was asking some hard questions because at thirty-eight years old, I really didn't and don't care what your favorite color is, or what you like to eat or watch on TV. Being upfront and honest about your life shows not only that you can tell the truth, but that you are comfortable with who you are and that you are self-aware and have done the work. I could've taken things a bit slower, but it was something that was important for me to know.

He responded with, "No, I did not." I let his answer sink in, then looked up at the sky and thought, "Thank God." He had said his marriage fell apart due to hidden resentment and because he and his wife married young. I believed him, I had no reason not to.

A few weeks later, I still couldn't shake a feeling. Something just didn't sit right with me. I questioned this superman of a human being on why his marriage ended. Again, he said he hadn't cheated on his wife. I believed him.

A week before Thanksgiving, I had my entire group of friends over, as I was so excited for them to meet Seth. They sat around the table asking questions, some silly, some more serious than others. The turning point of the night was when my friend Julie, who is very intuitive, asked a question about his ex-wife. The question seemed to ignite defensiveness; you could see his posture change. I started to sink down in my chair as the man who I was hoping to impress my friends with was getting grilled by them. As I sensed his discomfort, I sank at that moment a little deeper in my chair and I listened to what my gut was trying to say to me.

Why was he so defensive of the question around his ex-wife?

Why is he blaming his ex-wife for things if the divorce was mutual?

• • • •

Why do some of us find ourselves starving for a relationship, while others are perfectly content with being alone? How can we avoid heartbreak and pain? How can we predict what will work and what won't? How do we avoid relationship self-sabotage?

At some point we have all struggled with those questions in our lives. I have dear friends who never married, and they always ask me, "Will I be single forever?" Other friends have never married or are divorced, and they could not care less if they found someone or not!

Truthfully, after my divorce I found myself asking that same question. I don't want to be single forever. I like having a companion. I want to have someone to roll over to in the morning, laugh with, and even have the boring old what-are-we-going-to-have-for-dinner discussion. I wish I had a crystal ball that would tell me what's going to happen. I may say that, but then I remember a moment in church when the pastor talked about this.

She said, "God's ways are better than our Waze [a map app]." What she was trying to say was that if we had it our way, followed our Waze, we may be able to avoid potholes, and reroute around the traffic. However, in God's ways, we can't click "avoid this breakup" or "skip this painful memory." God's ways have us walking through our experiences and hardships, learning and growing from them. Also, think about how boring it would be to have our Waze. Sure, we could avoid heartache or repeated mistakes, always taking the easy path, but when we work through things we learn about ourselves and realize our strength.

As much as I would love to see the blueprint God has for my life, I never will. Only God knows whether I will be single forever. But I can say this: the odds of never finding love again are rare, at least in my fairytale brain. I think it comes down to putting yourself out there when you feel healthy and ready, whether you sign up for an app or go out to dinner with friends. You never know who you are going to run into.

I also believe in God's timing, that he will show us when it is right. I also believe that if you do the work, you will find a peace in yourself and won't keep thinking about it. That is where I found myself in my healthiest moment. My advice is to love yourself and be happy with your life and your journey. That is when God will make room for someone else to join you.

At the beginning of my divorce and even before that, in my late twenties and early thirties, I wondered if I would be single forever. It's hard to believe what we can't see. When I found happiness in myself, that question didn't weigh heavy on my heart. I felt I was enough. I was truly happy alone. I didn't need a man to define my worth—and I know no matter what happens in my love life in the present day, I will be okay with or without.

When I first started the conversation with my editor on writing a book post-divorce, she had mentioned that maybe we wait until I was happy in a relationship. Even though she meant it kindly, I said the biggest *no* ever. I told her how important it was for me to write this book while *not* in a relationship. My whole life my happiness has revolved around a man. If I was single, I was depressed. If I was in a relationship, I was "happy." The reality was that in both situations I was still unhappy. I told my editor how important it was to me to find happiness without the label of a relationship, and she got it. I knew that was the only way to find true freedom and happiness in my life. I knew that if I wanted to find a great love again, that it would take me falling in love with myself first.

Once you get to that place where you feel fine being alone, protect the incredible space that you have built for yourself that you love and where you feel safe. Don't let someone in just because you are alone or miss companionship. Don't let someone in just because you are starving. Let someone into that sacred space when they're deserving of it.

127

The Next Chapter

If you were in a relationship that ended, you were given the gift of being set free, so don't go back. When you meet someone, consider whether they truly fill your cup and whether they match the description of the person you told God you wanted. I wish I had known this when I met Seth, but, as I said before, that was God's way. That relationship taught me some valuable lessons, and one of them was I needed to take more time to choose wisely. That was a lesson I needed to learn in that moment, and I am glad I did. The best was yet to come for me.

This is your walk. Walk your life with God and be selective about who you let walk beside you. I found the greatest peace when I was alone with God, and it felt amazing. You won't be alone forever; you aren't alone now. God is, and has always been, with you. And you are with yourself. Love yourself in the way you want to be loved and never settle for less from someone else.

part three

Winter

Let the Light In

You intended to harm me, but God intended it for good
to accomplish what is now being done, the saving of
many lives.

—GENESIS 50:20

December

December arrived—the month I had been dreading since
I signed the divorce paperwork—and with it the holiday I
would always think about when I thought about my divorce.
Christmas Day when My Ex and I were going through divorce
paperwork I said, "You shouldn't get Christmas at all. Ever."
I was angry, really angry. When custody of the kids during
the holidays shook out, we decided that I would get them on
Christmas Eve and Christmas morning. At noon Christmas

Day they would leave to spend the rest of the year with My Ex. That arrangement wasn't what I wanted. It wasn't fair.

It wasn't fair.

It wasn't fair.

It wasn't fair.

Beginning December 1, "It wasn't fair" was on repeat in my head. The moment Christmas was around the corner, I was mourning the holiday. This was the first Christmas I would eat dinner alone since—ever. Like everything that first year after my marriage ended, the "first" anything was always the hardest to deal with. I wasn't ready to spend Christmas alone, nor did I want to face it.

• • •

Once my parents divorced, Christmas became my least favorite holiday. My time was always divided between so many different houses, with relatives feeling hurt if my visit wasn't long enough. I knew none of this was my fault, as I didn't make the decisions about where I would spend time and for how long. Nothing was up to me. I also hated the long car rides that really cemented the fact that my family wasn't intact, that my parents lived in different worlds, and that I was both the main event and a total afterthought. Being carted around on the holidays, especially Christmas, was a frustrating experience, as I felt powerless and had to perform for everyone.

I promised myself I wouldn't put my kids through that. If you had asked me why I didn't get a divorce from My Ex during the first revelations of his infidelities, a part of it was because of Christmas. I didn't want to put my kids through the same experience during the holidays like I had. And I didn't want to be away from them myself. I also didn't want to relive old childhood wounds or make my kids ever feel that same way. I had no choice but to come to terms with the truth: this first year was the new normal.

After my initial mourning period, I resolved to make the holiday special for my kids and to put on the brave face I'd worn many times throughout that year. Each day of December, leading up to Christmas Eve, I had fun Christmas activities planned. We'd see Santa, make gingerbread houses, and take a boat ride through the Grand Ole Opry to see the lights. These were all the things that we did as a family of four the year before, but this time I went the extra mile, to make some core memories for them and myself.

Sometimes I looked at the sparkling lights of the thirteen-foot tree in my home and I'd think about holidays past and be overcome with sadness, not the anger I thought I would feel. I thought our kids deserved better. They should be celebrating Christmas with their mom *and* dad. Maybe one day we could do this as a family. I let that thought in, then quickly reminded myself that we weren't there yet.

In our first December session, as I was bemoaning my current predicament, my therapist asked me what exactly I love about Christmastime.

I thought about it, then I said, "The lights."

She suggested I find something this season that felt like light. To decorate the house around that theme, to unabashedly "go toward lights." That would be a way to keep the magic of this season alive for me, and maybe even improve it in the process.

But that idea seemed like a Band-Aid. If I'm honest, I didn't want to decorate for Christmas that year. The first Christmas season with our new normal straight up depressed me. It brought up the false narrative that I failed as a mom and a former wife. For me, Christmas was ruined. A part of me thought that if I downplayed Christmas it might slip by without the magnifying glass on the fact that it would never be the same.

What about my kids though? They deserved the best Christmas ever and, it was clear to me after that therapy session, we all needed some light. So, I lit up the house like the character Clark Griswold does in *National Lampoon's Christmas Vacation*. I put a Christmas tree in every room, lights on the garland that wrapped around the curving banister of the entire main staircase, and little fairy lights around Christmas decorations that sat on shelves. I was determined to let the light in no matter what darkness I felt that December.

And you know what? Some of my favorite Christmas memories were made that year. Those are words I never thought I would say. The kids and I made Christmas ours. As the stockings were hung, we baked cookies and set them out for Santa, and we left out deer feed and carrots for the reindeer. I tucked in two very happy babies on the night before Christmas. Christmas morning came and went as fast as a child ripping wrapping paper off a toy; the countdown to noon felt like a ticking time bomb. When it was time for them to leave, I hugged Jace and Jolie as hard as I could, somehow managing to say, "Goodbye, my loves," the words I never wanted to say on Christmas Day. I cried the rest of the day.

My Ex called that afternoon and asked if I wanted to come over for dinner. I thought that was brave and kind of him. He knew what I must be going through, and I am sure he had been going through the same thing that morning, as he woke up on Christmas Day without our kids.

But I decided to say no. I couldn't do it. I decided to honor this new normal. I was going through a lot of feelings, processing this experience, and for today, this was enough. This was a start. I politely declined and let my tears wash away the day.

I wasn't supposed to have the kids back until the start of the new year. When My Ex asked if I wanted to come over for dinner on Christmas night, though, a door swung open in my mind for our family—maybe we could treat the holidays with a little bit of grace for the kids and each other. I remembered that when we were together, My Ex always wanted to go out for New Year's Eve. Now that he was single, I figured he would like to do so. I never liked going out for New Year's myself. I figured it wouldn't hurt to call and ask if he would be open to me taking the kids for New Year's Eve—no pressure.

"Absolutely," he said, and two days later, the kids were back with me.

* * *

Sometimes, in moments when you feel pushed to the edge, what you really need is to give yourself some grace. You can give yourself the thing you need whether it's forgiveness, patience, kindness, understanding, or love. You don't need to wait for those things to come to you, you can give them to yourself for free this very moment.

If that's difficult for you and you can't find a way do that for yourself yet, let me give you that gift now.

You are worthy of being loved. You are worthy of loving another, and one day you will. I know how that anxious feeling of desperate wondering about the future can paralyze and destabilize you, and how much you want to know that a new day will come. Will another love come for me? Will I move on? Will someone love me for who I am?

The nineteenth-century Baptist preacher Charles Spurgeon once wrote, "To trust God in the light is nothing, but to trust him in the dark—that is faith." Looking back, I can see that it's no coincidence that my house was full of Christmas lights that December. I was searching for the light in my life and struggling to have faith in the dark. I worried about what my children would think of me during the holidays. I worried about whether the divorce would damage them. I wondered if I would enjoy another Christmas morning knowing my children would leave. Would I ever get past this new hurdle? To trust God in these moments, with these questions going through my mind, was the ultimate test of faith.

I needed the most grace when I decided to file for divorce almost six months earlier. I gave myself grace and strength, and I walked away. This is the question I am asked the most by followers: How do you know when to leave a partner, a marriage, a job, or a situation? I know why everyone asks! It took me a long time to end the marriage, but the question about knowing when to go are deeper questions about what lies ahead once you do leave. The future is the unknown— which may be scary enough to keep you where you are until, as I've said, the pain of staying is worse than the fear of the unknown. Some of those questions might be: How will you deal with the regret of lost years? How will you handle the shame and disappointment? How do you not feel sorry for yourself?

The answer is grace.

Let's start with the first question, how do you know when to leave? Well, the literal answer is that you should leave when the strength to leave comes from you and you alone— not your friends, your therapist, or your dog. I remember asking my friends whenever My Ex would relapse, "How do I leave, what if he changes this time?" One friend said to me, "It doesn't matter how many times we tell you to leave. One day you will have had enough." I always wondered, after every relapse didn't kill me like I thought it would, what else I could I handle. The infidelities and lies kept piling up, and I still stayed. My friend just kept saying, "One day you will hit your breaking point."

Working on our marriage through years of betrayal was painful, but I have no regrets for staying as long as I did, be- cause I took the time to make the decision for myself. I didn't listen to my friends or my family. I listened to my heart and my gut. I wanted to give him another chance because I loved him. I loved my little girl. I loved my little boy. I couldn't fathom the idea of someone else holding my baby girl or taking my little boy to preschool. I didn't want to lose my family. I would have always questioned leaving if I left after My Ex's relapses in 2016 and 2019. Today I know that I did everything in my power to try to save the marriage. I fought endlessly to fight the good fight. Those were some of the hardest, most trying times of my life, but they also gave me the closure I needed to move on. That is what giving yourself grace—and letting the light in—is all about.

Perhaps you are in a relationship amid some hard years, and you aren't sure which direction your relationship is going to go. Maybe you have a suspicion that one day you will leave, or maybe you're just unhappy in this moment. Have faith in the dark. Have faith in yourself, not your partner. Be assured that one day you will know, unequivocally, where to go next. It's okay if that day isn't today or tomorrow or next year. One day you will know. Until then, let the light in and be at peace.

I had my moment of knowing that I had to leave when I physically couldn't try any longer. Trust me, knowing doesn't make leaving any easier, but you will know when it's time. It'll hurt like hell, but you will be ready to walk through fire to get out. So many times, I wouldn't leave My Ex because he would plead his case and say, "I'll never do it again." The idea that he would change and have a good relationship with someone else after I had worked so hard on the marriage was . . . Not. Going. To. Happen. I had shed so many tears in therapy, had spent so much time and money to fix the marriage, and there was no way in hell another woman was going to benefit from this new man. No way in hell do I want another woman raising my children. Those thoughts had me clinging on to the marriage for five years.

I needed those years! I am grateful for those years! Those five years clarified the kind of woman I am, that I believe in the people I love, that I champion and support them. That I am loyal and kind and would do anything for my children. I wouldn't trade that self-knowledge for anything.

That said, when I knew I'd had enough, I stopped caring whether My Ex was a better version of the mess he was for me for the next girl. I was done carrying the stress and weathering the emotional instability; I felt it in my body. I physically could not do to it any longer. That's when I knew I didn't want to be in the relationship any longer.

I look at it like God had been preparing me for this for years. He knew I had to take this route, that I had to move slowly. He knows my heart and my thoughts, and he knows how I do things, what makes me comfortable. He never gives you more than you can handle, so I knew that I could do it, even though there were days that I feared I couldn't.

Someday you will realize that everything you went through was a blessing in disguise. Stay down. Let your friends and family take care of you. Let them show you how special you are and give yourself time to heal. Things didn't work out the way you expected them to because you were being prepared for something even better. All the restless nights wondering why everything happened will finally make sense. Don't be surprised how quickly things in your life will move once you decide you want and deserve better. They say in the Bible we will reap a harvest if we don't give up. It won't be easy, but you are worth walking away from a situation that was trying to destroy you.

Give yourself grace. Let the light in.

A Fresh Start

Forgiving isn't something you do for someone else. It's something you do for yourself. It's saying, "You are not important enough to have a stronghold on me." It's saying, "You don't get to trap me in the past. I am worthy of a future."

—JODI PICOULT, *The Storyteller*

2022

January

"Happy New Year!!" I have never shouted those words so loud. It was a running joke with my friends that on New Year's Eve I would always cry. I used to say to them I never knew why. But I knew. I wasn't happy. Another year had ticked on by and I still wasn't where I wanted to be. Not relationally, not professionally, not emotionally. My therapist reminded me that the previous two New Year's I had called her from my closet crying after new discoveries that were found in my marriage. This New Year's, though, I wasn't hiding in a closet crying or calling my therapist. There was nothing more for me to find that would destroy me or rock my world. I didn't have to wear my detective hat or fear what land mine I would step on anymore. I was able to bury that last year. Last year. Words that let me put some past to rest. This was a new year. A happy new year. A year that hasn't been touched and can't be touched by My Ex. I felt power in that. A real fresh start.

* * *

How do you forgive someone who has ruined your marriage, your career, and your family? How do you forgive someone who has robbed you of your happily ever after, your Randy Travis "forever and ever amen"? How do you forgive someone who has spoken to you with the intention of hurting you? How do you forgive someone who hurt someone you love?

I used to struggle with forgiveness. Specifically, I would think: "I can't forgive, because I'll never forget." Unless you are blessed to step into the world of the movie *Eternal Sunshine of the Spotless Mind* and completely erase your memories, then this is the case: You will never forget. You will never forget the pain, the hurtful moments, and the agonizing emotions you went through, ever. That can be tough to hear, I know. I couldn't stop *remembering*, especially in the first year.

Those memories weighed so heavily on my soul that I felt like my past was weighing down my present.

I would remember the smell of My Ex's shirt. The feeling of his arms around me in our bed at night. The sound of him stomping around the house whenever he was mad at me. Making him laugh, his booming laugh that filled up a room. The sound of our babies laughing as he playfully wrestled with them. Sitting in our office together, revising and writing and rewriting our book, sharing secrets we had never told each other, getting inside each other's brains. That uncomfortable feeling sitting next to each other in a couple's therapy session. The way his face would turn when he felt attacked, when he got defensive. The way my body and mind would go light when I felt gaslit and blamed. Our kids and the two of us meeting together like four corners of a square falling in on ourselves in a family kiss. The good memories can hurt as much as the bad ones.

Here's what I know to be true: forgiveness is freedom. I really needed to forgive My Ex, not for him, but for me, so I could move on and let the anger go. Forgiving wasn't about excusing his actions, but making it possible for me to breathe easily again. I needed to forgive his past actions and let them go without taking my good memories with them. I didn't need to tell him I forgave him either. Forgiveness is for you. You shouldn't have to hold on to those memories and pain. More important, you shouldn't have to repeat them. If our thoughts are our realities, then the recurring slideshow of our bad memories can't possibly make for a healthy relationship today.

Where I think people get lost is that they think if they forgive, they are excusing someone's behavior, even validating it. That way of thinking is tough to overcome. I thought that if I held the bad memories in my mind forever, then someday I would have the justice I felt I deserved. I worried that if I forgot everything, I would be letting him win. But my marriage wasn't a crime story, with good guys and bad guys, cops, and judges. And worse, it seemed everyone had stopped caring about who did what to whom and when and where, except me. So here I was, replaying the good things and the bad things, analyzing them, accounting for them, nine months after our divorce because I hadn't yet forgiven My Ex and I hadn't been able to let go of all the hurt and anger. That's why I still held on to the details. I wanted to relay them to someone, someone who would understand how much I hurt and that what happened wasn't my fault.

If you find yourself doing the same thing . . . I get it. Believe me.

• • •

Forgiveness is about you. You are not excusing someone's poor behavior. By forgiving someone you are saying, "What you did really hurt me, and I'll never forget this pain, but I will forgive you," so that you can let go of the everyday struggle of living with the pain. It's about not letting what happened hold you down any longer or hinder your life experiences and days. In other words, by forgiving, you regain your power and potential for happiness. In the soft blanket of forgiveness, you no longer need to hold on to something that isn't your shame to carry.

I always thought I needed to hear "I'm sorry" to forgive someone. My Ex never apologized to me for the things he did to the full extent—and I wanted him to. In the end, I gave myself his apology. I wrote a letter from My Ex to myself and wept as I read it to my therapist in one of my sessions. The letter included all the things I wished he had said to me, all the apologies I needed to hear. Though the letter didn't come from him, the act of writing out everything I needed to hear was the healing I needed for my forgiveness.

If you never got your apology, I am sorry for the one who broke your trust. I am sorry for the one who took you for granted. I'm sorry you are hurting and that you lost someone you loved. I'm sorry for the ways they talked to you. You should have never known what it meant for a heart to be broken that way.

I once watched an interview with Sandra Bullock where she basically said that the people who hurt you don't care anymore, so why do you? Why are you letting what happened hold you down when those people moved on? Holding on keeps you in the pain of the past. You deserve to be set free. When you free yourself, you free everyone and everything around you that was once holding you down.

Don't let anyone stand between you and the door to freedom.

●　●　●

Forgiving My Ex took time, but forgiving myself took longer. I realized that the pain and anger I was holding on to wasn't about My Ex's indiscretions. It was the anger I felt toward myself about staying in a toxic relationship—that I wasted years of my life, resources, and time on a man who was not going to change and never wanted to, and that I let my children see us fight in unhealthy ways. I was angry that I was repeating old behavior patterns and ending up in the same kind of relationship.

Forgiving myself was harder than forgiving My Ex. I shut the door on grace for myself and repeatedly asked myself, *"How did I let that happen, again and again?"* *"Why wasn't I strong enough to close the door?"* Even though I don't regret the time it took to finally make the decision to leave, as I said earlier, I still had to forgive myself for allowing the toxic cycle to happen and for believing My Ex's promises when I never saw change. I had to forgive myself for believing someone's words over their actions.

To forgive myself, I had to open the door to grace again. I wanted my marriage to grow stronger and last, so why was I beating myself up for trying as long as I did? I walked away knowing I gave it my all and that there wasn't anything else I could have done. Maybe I could have walked away earlier, but those years are gone. I can't reverse the clock, but yes, with what I know now, I would have done things differently.

I got the gift of seeing my marriage play out, no matter how many years I struggled in the relationship. When things were difficult, I got the gift of knowledge and growth. I got the gift of another child. I battled to make things work and received the gift of peace.

I have found healing not only in forgiving My Ex, but forgiving myself, and acknowledging the gifts that I received as a result.

My biggest gift was the realization I was the one that needed to heal. God wants us to move forward in freedom. Instead of keeping yourself captive to others' actions toward you, actions that are not yours, look up and release what is not meant for you to carry anymore.

Giving myself the gift of grace changed my perspective.

It is hard, as I'm learning to live in a whole new way. I've been facing my greatest fears and finding they will not destroy me. I've been learning to trust my instincts and my heart. I've been learning to love myself first. People are going to make their choices no matter what I say or what I do, so what I did or do next comes from me. Seeing the gift in all the pain has helped me begin to forgive.

* * *

A true apology from My Ex owning all his past discretions would have been nice. But his validation is something I only thought I needed. The only way to get what you need without getting what you need is through God. Pray for healing. I started by praying that I wanted to forgive My Ex and forgive myself. I would repeat this mantra: "I want to forgive. I want to forgive."

Soon, "I want" turned into "I am," that is, "I am forgiving him, I am forgiving myself." Eventually, forgiveness became a part of my actions, as easy as breathing.

I am at a place now where I don't expect or need an apology

anymore. I have found healing not only in forgiving My Ex, but forgiving myself, and acknowledging the gifts that I received as a result.

• • •

Sometimes we want to hold on to the past in our relationships because there is a chance of getting back together. Forgiveness can feel like panic, an absence of hope for the future: "Oh, no. It's over. Is it *really over?*"

You might get back together with someone, but you will never be able to go back to how it was. If you're willing to forgive and stay, you will have to create a new relationship. There must be a new beginning, a new foundation for the relationship. This was where My Ex and I failed in our relationship.

In January, with the new energy of calm and rationality between us, there were things I wanted to discuss in order to put them behind me. But I knew I would be met with resistance. He wanted a fresh start as badly as I did. He didn't want to be reminded of all the hurtful things he did the years prior. I knew there would be a time when we could share our feelings of past resentment and hurt, but January 2022 was too fresh. We both were so hungry for a new year that bringing up any past would hinder any progress we made as coparents.

Our couple's therapist told us an analogy one time that always helped me when it came to healing. He told us to picture that My Ex was driving a car and crashed the car so horribly that my injuries included losing both my legs. He looked at

My Ex and said, "You wouldn't just tell her to move on and forget about it would you? She lost her legs."

All healing requires time and grace. You will have to sit with the damage of your car crash to see what pieces you can pick up and what you may have to walk away from. And that's when you must be thankful—you survived.

• • •

I can't help but think our babies were what My Ex and I did the best. Things weren't perfect and we had some big fights in front of them, but as far as parenting goes, we were on the same page. I'll take that as a win, right? I must also look at my reality. In my experience of our relationship, we were doing a lot of things that worked for both of us. We checked in at night, we made time for each other. We enjoyed playing games together. If I'm being honest, after our divorce, I used to miss sitting around our poker table and playing Risk with him or kicking his butt in Bananagrams. There was a feeling of love when we played games. It's almost like the games he played in our relationship were only off the table when it was just the two of us, actually seated at the poker table, rolling the dice, on the same page about the rules, going head-to-head. Sadly, those were probably the most honest moments we had together.

They say addicts can compartmentalize with the best of them. Though My Ex wasn't honest in our relationship in many ways, there were still small honest moments at the poker table some nights, and I'll take that as a win. It's hard to look at pictures when I was pregnant with Jolie or Jace and not think, "Oh, that's when he was sleeping with . . ." or "Yup, that's the day when I found this." In a way the knowing taints the memory for me, but I choose to go with the truth of the moment: I was pregnant, and my husband was presenting a certain kind of person to me. The beauty, love, and caring were real in my experience of that moment. To consider what was real for him would only send me down a deep hole; I'll never know.

I loved all the therapy we did, but I often wonder if we dragged it out for too long, so that it ultimately became counterproductive. That really comes down to me though. I wasn't strong on my boundaries. I would let things slide or go because I wasn't ready to end the marriage. I wasn't ready to open my eyes. Thinking back, my stronghold on our relationship might have been what killed us.

My therapist would say, "No, Jana, your ex's choices were the reason your relationship ended." That may be largely true, but I know he started to feel like a prisoner. I was so afraid of losing my family that I dug my nails in deeper to protect myself from getting hurt and to prevent him from hurting me again. Granted, my reactions were based on his actions so I try to not blame myself for him doing what he did, but I did hear a lot of times, "If you didn't do this, I wouldn't do that." Gaslighting at its finest, I know, but hearing it so many times I started to think if I was only more lenient then maybe he wouldn't cheat. Now, I feel like I can sympathize with My Ex on how he felt like he couldn't do anything.

He felt like he could never go out with his friends because a place might look too much like a club, and I would freak out. Maybe he just wanted to smoke a cigar with his friends, but I was terrified of another woman slipping her number in his pocket and him following up with it like he did on his bachelor party. I was scared, and he felt like he couldn't breathe.

Granted, I had let certain boundaries go overtime, but whenever I'd discover another infidelity or lie, he would be suited up again for another stay in a marital straitjacket. Some would say if he didn't lie and cheat, then he wouldn't need to be restrained. That's true, but the problem was he was so deep in the hole he had dug for himself, I can accept now that he couldn't get out and he knew it. So might as well keep digging the hole deeper. He would ask me, "How long are you going to be this way?" I always said, "Until you show me consistent behavior." But inconsistency, I came to realize, was part of his personality. I had married an inconsistent person.

I am lucky not to have an addiction, but I empathize with those that do. I can't imagine being powerless to something. I can't imagine something having such a stronghold over you that you would choose to risk everything to have it, including your family. To that point, My Ex could never say to me, "I'll never do this again."

When we got divorced, he told me that he knew that I would always have a leg up in the relationship as long as his hole was so deep. He said he knew he would always be looking up at me.

The Next Chapter

I asked him, "Why not just break up with me if that's what you thought? Why keep trying if you knew you couldn't and didn't want to climb back out?"

He simply said, "It was hard on me too."

Not every question has an answer, and we must learn to accept that.

Tribe

If you want to recognize the lies . . . study the truth.

—PASTOR KEVIN QUEEN

February

In February, I wanted to give myself over to God fully, so I felt I was being called to get baptized.

I wanted to tell God I was ready to walk with him as a new woman. I wanted to make that commitment to myself and to let the world know.

As I let the water wash over me and saw my little Jolie and all my friends cheering me on, I just kept thinking, "God is so good. I am here, I am alive, and I just got through one of the hardest nine months of my life and he never left me." My sign from God? When I came up from the water, the singer in the band was singing, "In the name of Jesus there is heal-ing," and I knew he was in the room with me. My baptism was my battle cry. It was my hands-up moment to say, "I surrender to you, Jesus. I'm here to listen and to honor you and to seek you."

Since that day, and for the first time in my life, even on days when I'm the only person in my house, I have not been alone.

Back in April, when I had my final fight with My Ex, my entire group of close friends, also known as the Queendom, was capital D, Done. They were ready for another capital D, Divorce.

When you're going through a divorce, you discover who your true friends are. In my case, I was fortunate to have a beautiful group of women rise up around me.

They protected me.

Cared for me.

Celebrated me.

And they didn't give in to my bullshit.

My friends have always given me the gift of clarity. They saw the marriage as it was. To trust them was to trust the truth of the situation I was living, but I couldn't quite see it. Be-cause I was hopeful. Because I was emotional. Because I had baggage and blinders.

Think about it this way. If you get stung by a bee, it doesn't help to blame the bee. A bee is a bee, and bees sting. That bee isn't going to change into a butterfly tomorrow, no matter how much we want or believe that it will. But we all want to believe the bee in our life is a butterfly in disguise!

That is where my friends come in. They don't judge me or

blame me for wanting to see the good in someone. Instead, they help me see the truth, gently and compassionately.

Whenever I would share what was going with My Ex, one friend, she would always quote Maya Angelou, who once said, "When someone shows you who they are, believe them the first time."

My response was always, "Yeah, but—" and I would come up with something he did or said that would justify staying in the relationship.

When something would happen again, she would patiently say, "He is showing you who he is, believe him."

And one day, I did.

•   •   •   •

The friend that surprised me the most with her unwavering support was Kristen. I met Kristen when I was on radio tour for "I Got the Boy" and we became instant friends. She is a Michigan girl who bleeds love. Even her daughter's name is Love. In 2017, My Ex and I had just reconciled and decided to try living in Los Angeles for a fresh start. Kristen came into town with her daughter to be with Jolie and me while I continued to try to pick up the pieces of my marriage.

One night, I had a fight with My Ex. I don't remember exactly what we fought about, but I'm sure I was trying to beat into his brain that I was hurting and didn't trust him, and that I didn't understand why he couldn't be empathetic instead of getting defensive and mad at me.

All My Ex heard was shame, and with him, where there

was shame there was anger. At times, due to past incidents, his anger would scare me. This time, I ran downstairs and slipped under the kitchen table. Kristen heard me and came out of her room to find me.

She said, "Friend, are you okay?"

I said I wasn't and started crying. Without skipping a beat, Kristen was under that table with me.

No one knew the extent of some of the arguments My Ex and I used to have and how volatile they would get. When I started to say, "I'm so sorry," she stopped me and said, "Nope, don't do that." She loved me even through the mess of life, and she loved me and My Ex regardless of the thirty minutes we stayed under that table. When the final discovery of My Ex's infidelity came to a head, Kristen texted me: "It's time." I was blown away, and at that moment I knew my marriage was over because even the most forgiving of friends was done too.

Julie is another friend who has been a constant in my life since the beginning of my relationship with My Ex. She knew we struggled, and she helped me see the other side and have empathy for him. Julie is the part of Queendom that helps us look at ourselves rather than the other person in a relationship situation. She reminds us that people's feelings are their feelings; all we can do is hold healthy boundaries. She is my spirit guide.

Pamelyn is not only my neighbor, but she has practically become a sister wife. Her husband is out of town a lot, so we are raising our girls together, and she is my Pittsburgh Pam when I need her to be—she is fiery and takes no shit. She has given me the gift of seeing the beauty in being alone and not settling for less. Within a few hours of my phone call to the divorce attorney, she cleared My Ex's clothes out of our closet and organized mine so I could walk in and not see empty hangers.

Then there is Sara. Sara makes me laugh harder than anyone I know. Thanks to her, I found out about everything that had been going on with My Ex from day one. I had confided in her about some of his behavior, and she suggested I look at the phone bill. So, when in Orlando about to play a show, I looked and saw dozens of numbers that, when Googled, were not places that a married man should be dialing. My Ex was staying at our neighbors during our first split, and Sara was the girl who marched up the street to see him. She brought along a sixty-by-thirty-inch wedding photo of us and said to him, "How could you mess this up?" I'll never forget sweet little Sara carrying that Shutterfly framed canvas as she hiked up Ironwood Drive. I'm pretty sure I took a knife to that canvas when she brought it back.

157

•   •   •

During my divorce all those girls, my Queendom, saved me. They listened while I said things like "I'll never be loved again." "My family is ruined." "How did this happen?" over and over again. They lay down with me as I cried. They fed me the first two weeks after My Ex left, and they held my hand until I was on the other side.

I can't stress enough how much I needed my Queendom

and how impactful their friendship was for me in my darkest times. They took shifts to check on me. They all know me so well that after some time, I would withdraw and shut them out. When I did that, they would show up unannounced and talk me off the ledge I was standing on. I'm forever indebted to my Queendom; they showed me more love than I've ever felt from any man. All they have wanted for me was to believe and love myself in the way they love and see me. It took a few years, but for the first time in my life, thanks to the words they spoke over me time and time again, I love myself as my Queendom loves me. I see myself how my Queendom sees me. The Queendom's text thread, especially when I was dating, were almost more fun than the dates I'd gone on themselves. My friends know I haven't been 100 percent honest in the past due to me wanting them to like the guy, but this go-around, they know it all.

Some days the thread is like an episode of *The Kardashians* you don't want to miss. We all bring our different personalities and there is so much joy that comes from talking with them and laughing. There is nothing better than being in a judgment-free zone where your friends will call you out yet still love you and be there for you. There will be a season when I'll be needed as much as I've needed them, and I'll be under that table with them.

Life is not meant to be lived alone. We are not meant to carry all our pain, thoughts, joys, and hopes alone. These things are meant to be shared, celebrated, and held. Find someone other than your partner to share in your life. Men will come and go, but a Queendom lasts a lifetime.

• • •

Having so many friends taught me how to be a friend to my-self during the hardest year.

Let me flip this around for a second. What would you tell your friend that is going through what you're going through today? What advice would they give to you? What would you tell your daughter if she was going through this? That's the kind of friend you need to be to yourself.

Unleash the weight, the heaviness, and embrace the free-dom. Even if that means you might be alone for a little while. I can promise you the fifteen years that my mom was single after my parents divorced was better than the lies and affairs she probably would have had to contend with. She also would have missed out on the love she has now, who treats her better than my dad ever could have then (sorry, Dad).

Love yourself enough to not stay in a relationship because you're afraid that you won't be loved again. You are already loved. You just need to let it in. I know that's easier said than done.

Here are some things that helped me get out of that rut:

Speak your thoughts out loud. I must've said, "Who would ever love me or want to be with me?" at least two hundred times.

Find the friends that will sit with you 201 times and speak truth into you.

Pray. You are and will never be alone. That was the most healing thing I did: embracing God and the knowledge that he will never hurt me or lie to me. He will always be by my side.

The Next Chapter

When you can let that sink in, there is a sense of peace and comfort in knowing you don't need another person to validate you or that you are lovable.

Finally, the thing I want you to do at that moment *and* right now is give yourself time. In time you will realize getting out of a bad situation is a lot better than staying or settling just because you're afraid of what might be out there.

Let me tell you what is out there. A stronger, healthier you. A wiser, braver you. A healed, loving you. You will find you again, and you will love you on the other side.

part four

Spring

Grow

I survived because the fire inside me burned brighter
than the fire around me.

—JOSHUA GRAHAM, *Fallout*, "NEW VEGAS"

March

As winter turned into spring, I knew I needed to confront my
relationship with Seth.

Seth had ruptured something in me—I was fed up. I was
over it. His lying. My finding things out. The familiar anxious
feelings from my past. Then my anxiety started turning into
rage. What was wrong with me? Why was I so incapable of
finding something that would last, that would feel comfortable, easy, and fun, and just be fine? And why was I staying in
something when I knew it wasn't right? Why was I worried

about what people would think if I had another "failed" relationship? Why was that my reason for staying?

All this rage manifested in distant memories of My Ex coming back to the present, and the resentment came boiling up.

Let me back up. Seth and I had booked a trip for spring break, and even though the wheels of our relationship felt like they were coming off, we packed our passports and swallowed our emotions and off we went. Maybe everything would repair itself with the help of a beach and some good times.

The delayed planes and long layovers were just the start of a not-so-happy ending to the vacation. I was boiling inside. I could feel it, he could feel it, and all I kept doing was trying to not let my kids feel it. I was upset because I realized that I messed up, that I shouldn't have brought the kids here. I was dragging my kids into a mess I single-handedly created because I wanted them to have a picture-perfect family. There I was again, repeating a pattern to give them what I didn't have. Instead of leaning into the situation and trying to see the positive side of the trip, all I could feel was that I failed them. I've always said that I'm an okay actress and an okay singer, but I'm a great mom. How could I say that now? I was so mad at myself. That entire trip I knew it was over. He knew it was over. Why were we beating a dead horse?

While Seth and I were together for Christmas and the holidays, my suspicion that his relationship with his ex-wife hadn't ended on good terms was correct. The truth found me, and then a month later I looked through his phone for more confirmation and I found more than I was looking for. Side note: if you have to look through someone's phone to find truth or answers, you're not in the right relationship. I vowed to never again be in a relationship where I ever felt the need to look through a phone. There should be trust, and how your partner is treating you shouldn't even give you a reason to look. You shouldn't have to be a detective in your relationship. You should feel safe and without a doubt trust that your partner is honoring you and your relationship. And remember, when your gut tells you to go snooping, you most likely will be on the other end of finding things that could really hurt.

It didn't matter to me what happened with Seth and his ex; after all, I wasn't exactly perfect. What bothered me was that he had lied to me when I asked him, point blank, for the truth. From that point on, the same old cycle that had been set into motion by my relationship with My Ex began. Seth was still someone that I wanted close to me, but I didn't trust him. That combination made me anxious, worried, needy, clingy, unsure, and insecure. But it also made me mad, distant, suspicious, and miserable. Worse? The same thing happened with Seth that had happened for seven years with My Ex—I became consumed with not wanting to look like a failure, and I worried I wouldn't find anyone better.

*   *   *

I don't like to live with regrets, but I wish I could go back to November and stop myself from rushing into that first relationship post-divorce. I wish I took my time to let all the "firsts" of that divorced year come and go, and do it on my own. I experienced big emotions that year and my body needed to feel them, and my tears needed to wash them away. Instead, I let myself fall into someone else's arms, and that wasn't a safe place. Seth made me feel guilty and ashamed for still having big emotions around the fallout of my marriage. One time I came home to an empty house, and he asked me why I was crying. I told him, "Sometimes it's just hard and I miss my family" as I sat there wiping tears. He said nothing and left my house. I couldn't believe he didn't come sit next to me or even try to console me, but in that moment, I knew my emotions were too much for him, so I tried to cover them up after that. I didn't want to be "too much" for this person, but I've learned that you will never be too much for the right person, and when you are going through something life-changing like this, you need time to grieve all those firsts.

I would have ended it with Seth myself, but I was so stuck in the hamster wheel of my past traumas and shame. I wanted the relationship to work because I wanted to prove to myself that I had grown. After he ended it, I wondered what exactly I had to show for the last year. Another failed relationship, and where was the silver lining? Where was the growth?

When things ended with Seth, my therapist said, "At least you figured it out sooner and left. That's your growth." I looked at her a little awkwardly and said, "Yeah, but I repeated some bad patterns. I didn't listen to my gut or pay attention to the red flags." She stopped me mid-sentence and said, "Yes, but you figured it out in three months, not three years."

She paused, and I let that sit with me.

"That is growth, Jana," she said.

• • •

Nothing will make you more fed up with yourself and your same old shit than having the same feelings in a three-month relationship that you had in a six-year relationship. And the same ones you had in the relationship before that and before that. It was infuriating to have to reckon with myself again, this time with a heaping plate of rejection to go along with it.

But nothing ignites a next chapter quite like being fed up with wasted time.

Reaching the finish line of that relationship in March, I finally committed to doing some of the hardest work I've done in my life. It has led me to peace, and I found that in my silence. I have found a love for my time, and I value it more than any random past Wednesday date or trying to fit a square peg into a round hole. That's a double pun, indeed, because I had dated a few squares!

• • •

Here's where I failed myself and my worth. I stayed with Seth when I knew he had lied to me and that he was capable of doing it again because it was more than just one lie when we were together. I needed a complete tune-up. I give a lot of grace to a lot of people, but I have never been true to the boundaries I wanted in a relationship. If you were to write a list of what you want in your relationship, what would it look like? Are you making excuses as to why you are turning your head on some of the boundaries? I thought, "Well, he is great in this area," or "All the love notes he writes show he loves me, and he says he won't lie again." The problem is that when you make your list and you set boundaries for a relationship, not lying to the other person should be at the top. It is for me, yet I give grace and benefit of the doubt when I'm lied to, or I choose to believe their words over their actions.

I have always struggled with that piece though. I truly want to give so much grace, and I know it's not easy to be honest at times. While I'm giving grace for people, I'm in return disrespecting myself. I'm also letting that person know that they can disrespect me too. I also go to the place where I say, "I have lied before, so why should I ever cast judgment if it's harder for some people too." The problem is, my marriage with My Ex left me with some major trust issues. Lying is a big no. In fact, I pleaded with Seth to be honest with me. I don't need perfection, just honesty. I realized when I wasn't telling the Queendom about him lying to me, I knew things weren't headed in a right direction. I wanted them to like him, so I hid things from them.

And there we go: I just lied by omission. I didn't want to hear what I already knew.

Where else did I go wrong? I was forcing something because I wanted the fairy tale, the perfect family ideal held in my mind to be real, just like I did with My Ex. But as the Queendom always reminded me, the reality of all situations is right in front of you. People show you who they are. It's up to us to believe them. Actions and words sync up when people are showing you who they are. It's almost as if God knew I needed Seth out of my life too. I feel like God said, "You can't end this, so I'm going to do it for you." He knew I still didn't believe in myself enough or value myself enough and he knew what was going on behind closed doors.

What else can I own? Was I passive? Did I anxiously hold on to him and that relationship? Yes. Now my friends would come to my defense and say he lied to me from the jump and with my past, it makes sense that I would go back to old patterns. Sure, I see that, but where is that growth on my end? Isn't looking through yet another guy's phone not the biggest sign in the world that this wasn't the right relationship for me? Wasn't I back where I just left off? I wanted that pretty family picture so badly that I clung on to something that felt familiar in my previous trauma bond and I reverted to old behaviors.

. . .

If there's one thing my past taught me, it is to value my time. My time is precious. Raising my kids and working as a single mom 70 percent of the time makes me not only appreciate my time but value it as sacred.

I think so often in my past I would give up my time to please others. If I were to peel it back even more in my marriage, I think I gave all my time to My Ex because I was afraid if I wasn't spending my every moment with him, then he would cheat on me. The less time my husband wanted with me, the more I wanted to spend with him. I wanted to devote so much of my time and energy to him and the kids that I not only put some restraints on our relationship, but I lost time for myself, my time to enjoy doing things I wanted to do, or as I look back, time I needed to devote to myself.

The Next Chapter

The time spent alone post-divorce has shown me how truly sacred that alone time is. I can hear my thoughts better. I can rest in the safety of what I've created, and I can hear God more clearly. Those three things have become a staple for me in my time.

On one of my alone nights in March, I wondered about loneliness and why I hadn't been able to work through it. It's okay to feel lonely from time to time, and that's normal when you are single but, like everything else, loneliness doesn't last forever. You will not be alone forever. You will not be single forever. You will not have your alone time forever. Why not cherish it?

At that moment of being lonely, I asked myself, *"What do I want to do?"*

The reality is I can do whatever I want. I don't need to check up on anybody or give them my status. I don't need to ask someone what they want to do. I get to do whatever in heck I want to do.

I could binge *Sex and the City* without having to listen to the annoyed grunts of a man (although I swear men love that show, whether they want to admit it or not), or I could go to bed at seven p.m. and have cereal for dinner if I wanted to. If you're in the lonely single girl season, cherish it, because it won't last.

I said exactly that to a friend. Fifty-five and divorced, she had said, "I will be alone forever, and I'll never find love." Now she's seeing someone and more in love that she ever thought was possible. I did a happy dance and called her and reminded her that no matter what age or what season we are in, love is found, and seasons change. I say all that to remind you to value your time and embrace where you are in this moment. If you're in a relationship, then that's the exploration work you get to do to really ask for what you need.

The greatest lesson I learned from my last marriage—and then my relationship with Seth—was that being together all the time might not be the best idea. Having your own time is valuable, not only for you, but for the marriage.

I'm going to challenge you to do something. Call a friend or a family member and plan a two-night getaway. No kids, no boyfriend, no spouse. Just you and your friend. If you want extra credit points, go away alone with a journal and some hiking boots and get lost with yourself. We are all on a mission of greater understanding and healing—and that starts with us.

•   •   •   •

The older I get the more I realize that I don't have to say yes to things. My circle of friends gets smaller, sure, but not because I'm losing friends. My time is spread thin, and I know what I can give, what I can't, who I want to give that extra time to. Be mindful of those who seem to take up too much of your time draining your energy and leaving you on empty. Since you create your sacred space, you get to choose who can come in. For me, it's God, my kids, my Queendom, and my relationship. Everything else is let in when I have time and energy for it. That's not selfish, it's being self-aware. I'm a better mom when I'm not spread thin, and I know I'm a better friend when I'm present and can listen actively to their stories instead of spacing out because I'm exhausted. Be selfish with your time—it's yours. We all have obligations, jobs, kids, husbands (well, not all of us), and other things that require our attention. What do you want to do with what's left after all of that?

Your next chapter doesn't have to be stressful, with not enough time in the day. Maybe there are a few things weighing you down that you can let go of. Instead of taking that one extra call, go for a walk so that you have time to hear your own thoughts. Your next chapter in your life will be based on how you value your time because we all know what it feels like to carry too much. When our life is over, no one is going to be evaluating our time on Earth based on how much money we made or how successful we were. What matters is how well we loved ourselves and in turn our capacity to love others.

If you're anything like me, you give yourself the least amount of grace for your healing and where you are at in your life. Falling back into unhealthy patterns is an easy way to beat up on yourself. Instead of doing that, give yourself some understanding. Say, "Of course I did." Take a look at what you went through, whether it's a childhood trauma and negative messages you received growing up, or a breakup that caused you a great deal of pain and confusion. Those patterns hold the key to understanding yourself better. They give a voice to the unhealed parts of yourself. Treat yourself with kindness and give yourself grace that we can't fix patterns overnight.

Show me one person that saw a pattern and didn't repeat it at least once.

Instead of beating yourself up for doing the same thing

again by loving the same kind of man again or repeating patterns you promised you wouldn't, give yourself grace and say out loud, "AFGO." What is "AFGO?" I'm glad you asked ☺. It's "A Fucking Growth Opportunity."

What are you going to do about the fact you repeated an unhealthy pattern? You are going to grow. That's what you are going to do. You are going to take on the challenge and dig deep into why you are doing it again.

Jesus died for our sins, so we didn't have to be perfect. And we are not. What you did to survive may have been essential at the time, but now take the missed opportunities or broken hearts to do something different. The truth is we repeat what we don't repair. and if we don't repair, we are then going to bleed all over the people that didn't cut us.

• • • •

Paraphrasing Michelle Obama, "When people go low, you go high." You know the truth, and you walk away with dignity and your head held high. As the Bible says, "When the foundations are being destroyed, what can the righteous do?" (Psalm 11:3). Look inside yourself and ask God what he wants you to say. I promise he won't take you back down to the level of those that speak with intent to hurt. Being the bigger person in the end always makes you feel better. But trust me, I know the feeling of wanting to fight to be heard, understood, and loved. Ask yourself, though, what the price is—and whether it's worth it. Is it worth it? I say no. In my experience, it's more than likely that person will never

173

see your side. Like my therapist says, "Don't go back to the same well to drink poison when you know the well hasn't changed." The truth is, I never would have stayed with the men I did if I had taken the time to truly heal and love myself. I would have acted when I saw the red flags, rather than accepting lies and disrespect. If you're new out of a relationship sometimes taking that extra beat to process the pain and hurt before covering it up with glitter might work better in your healing journey.

· · ·

When my relationship with Seth ended, I asked myself what I was so upset about. That I was alone again? That I didn't listen to my gut? That I didn't love myself enough? That I didn't learn my lesson from the time before? That I didn't stop it when I should have?

Yes. Yes. And a big hell, yes.

I used to think being alone meant I was weak, or not worthy enough to have someone around. Now I see being alone as a place and time to find myself, learn about myself, be still, and lean into my faith. Feeling you're okay when you're alone is a foundation for being on steady ground with yourself. What you find out about who you are when you are alone is going to be yours and only yours. You get to create your own home. So today, being alone is a gift. Try to find the beauty in that even on the days when you struggle to be by yourself.

Stand Up

If I keep doing what I've always done, I'll keep getting
the same results I've always gotten.

—12 STEPS SLOGAN

April

As March rounded the corner on April, the fresh wound of
my drawn-out breakup with Seth was taking up most of my
headspace. I was days away from running in a half marathon
when Seth finally said the words, and we broke up for good. I
wanted to withdraw from the race so badly, but there wasn't
a chance in hell I wasn't going to run. I needed to prove to
myself that I didn't need him to run with me. That I could do
it on my own.

The morning of the race I was sick to my stomach. I guess

God knew all along that I needed to run that race alone, that I've needed to run alone for a lot of reasons and for a long time. The marathon was about to become more than a race for me.

I had two girlfriends with me the morning of the race. They knew I had had flown in from a show earlier that week and only slept a few hours the night before, so my whole body was out of whack. I was tired, had puffy eyes, and really hadn't eaten enough the week of the race. When I got to mile three, I lost it. Mile three. Just to be clear, there were still ten more miles to go. I kept looking around me at the massive crowd of runners, the Nashville sun beating down on us as we approached a less-than-forgiving hill. At that moment, my throat closed up, and I started to gasp for air.

"I can't do this," I said to my friend Emily, who was running alongside me at a painfully slow pace for her in a show of support. I dropped my twelve-minute-mile pace to a slow walk as I continued to hyperventilate and repeating, "I can't do this, I can't do this."

I kept thinking about how I was supposed to be running this race with my boyfriend. I was supposed to be happy and hitting a milestone with him. I was not supposed to be in this bad place again.

As we walked, I replayed the breakup to Emily. Hearing her say things like "Yeah, Jana, that's not okay," or "You deserve better," were like little chants I needed to be like "Yeah, f— this, I got this." But what really did the trick was not letting my mind win for the first time in my life. For years, I have let my fears hold me back from things I've wanted to do or

176

accomplish. I've let my mind warn me of an anxiety attack or come up with a list of negative what-ifs if I continue to do something.

Suddenly, I knew this was going to be my defining moment. I had the power to change my thoughts and let this race be the first step in not only healing but letting the shame messages and doubts of fears and anxiety fade away. It was also knowing at that moment that I wasn't truly alone, and that I didn't need a man to get me to the finish line. I always thought to be happy or accomplish something, I needed a man by my side because it validated my worth. Wrong.

"Okay, let's do this."

Emily looked at me, then said, "If we need to stop again, it's okay, but we are finishing this."

Knowing she was there for me, no matter if it took us two and a half hours or five, gave me so much peace. The next ten miles, I did a lot of talking myself down from the bridge and talking to God and focused on my breathing. I even belted out "Goodness of God" by the incredible CeCe Winans. When I got to mile eleven, I could feel the emotions start to flow through my body, and when I stepped across that finish line, I let them all out. I did it. I pushed through and let the heaviness of the last few months wash away. At the finish line were my two kids with handmade signs. I had texted My Ex earlier that week saying it would mean a lot if the kids could be there. I even arranged for a sitter to take them, so he didn't have to be inconvenienced. It was his weekend, and he had every right to say no. It was not lost on me that when I crossed the finish line, I not only saw my two precious kids, but also My Ex.

One year ago, I wouldn't have asked him for anything, and I bet you a year ago he wouldn't have done anything for me. We in a way were at our own finish line. Our own relational end of the race war.

. . .

Though a year post-divorce My Ex and I were good, I was at a crossroads. I felt it in my soul. I was feeling lost, frustrated that the same patterns were playing out on repeat in my life. Right after My Ex and I separated, I had wanted to go somewhere to work on myself, but I thought my weekly therapy sessions were enough, and I was tired of doing "the work." To be honest I had spent a lot of money on countless hours of therapy with My Ex so the thought of doing anything more than that just felt heavy. I had grieved. I was tired. I wanted to be free. I wanted to be done. I wanted to move on from my marriage and just start again.

The problem was that I hadn't fixed my core issues, the deep messages about myself that I had held on to for years were still locked away in my body. I wasn't making progress in that way, and I knew I needed to dig deeper into my work. I knew the relationship issues weren't about the men I was choosing. The problem wasn't them. It was me. I was the common denominator. If I were healthy, I wouldn't choose these men, let alone stay in these damaging relationships. I saw the pattern: At first, I would blame them and say I was blindsided (in one case, I think I truly was), but the truth is, I saw the red flags and ignored them. The reality in that was I was too unhealthy to make the right choices with my heart, so I fell back into the same patterns, following the same beliefs about relationships, and listening to the negative messages about myself I have been believing my entire life. It was the exact same cast, just a different name and face.

I went to Onsite Workshops in 2011 after another failed trip down the aisle. It's where I began to look at my childhood traumas, my relationship with God, and my self-esteem. I remember having a profound response to the way my childhood influenced the way I react to people and why I stayed in certain situations. Yet here I was almost ten years later—doing the same thing with the same men, acting the same way, and believing the same lies about myself.

If I'm honest, it was one of the darkest times of my life. I had hit my lowest low. Even after my divorce I didn't feel this low. It's hard to admit what I'm about to write; in fact, I have only admitted this to my therapist.

The week after my breakup with Seth, I was spiraling. I had all the new facts around his past lies, the lies when we were together and I knew he wasn't the right person for me, but I was feeding into the social media accounts, seeing the hate and articles from his "tell all" to the press that spread hurtful lies. I even tried to get him back with emails saying, "I'm over my past and I've healed," just as I had begged the physically abusive man I was with when I was nineteen. I had completely lost myself. I pleaded with a publication to not run the story, as I had "proof that he lied." I had sent the editor all the information and her response was, "You can post that to your social, and I'll cover it." I yelled on the phone saying,

"But I just showed you proof he lied, how can you still run his story?" I learned that day, some people don't care about the full truth. They care about the drama. But this was my life, and I wasn't bulletproof. It hurt and I wanted so badly to prove my case, but when they go low you go high.

Bawling, I sat down on my bed, then grabbed my gun case out of my night-table drawer. I opened it and stared down at that gun in my hands and cried the loudest I ever have. I wanted the noise to stop. I wanted my brain to stop. I wanted the messages to stop. I just wanted it all to stop. The noise was unbearably loud—voices from the media; the hate from those who didn't know me, the truth, or my heart; and my need for love—and I needed to shut it all off.

Later, when I confessed what happened to my therapist, I told her I would never ever take my life, but I needed the voices to stop. I needed my brain to stop ruminating, to stop playing out the scenarios of my past. I continued to say I love my kids more than anything in this world and that I would never take my life, but I had to own up to the fact that I did grab the case and open it because I was desperate. I was crying out for help. I was crying out to myself to stop the cycle.

In the moment, though, I put down the gun and called my friend Miles Adcox who owns Onsite Workshops and told him I needed help. He called me that afternoon and said I could come the next day. I don't think I've ever driven as fast to a place as I did there.

Arriving at Onsite, I wasn't sure how I would feel about being there. When we were writing *The Good Fight*, My Ex went to Onsite to work on some of his issues for three days.

When he returned, we wrote the chapter entitled "To Tell the Truth." But the truth was that he met someone there and cheated on me with her the entire time that he was supposed to be doing his own therapeutic intensive work. That event at Onsite was the reason I finally filed for divorce. Going back to the place where My Ex was unfaithful was a sick twist in my storyline, but I wasn't going to let it get in the middle of the healing that I knew had to take place.

When I pulled into Onsite, which is about an hour and a half outside of Nashville, I was filled with emotions. The rolling mountains and the cottages that line the property set you up for peace, but my mind was racing. My first thought was, *"How am I here again?"* After all, this was my third time. The first time was ten years earlier, when I did work on self-love, and then again with My Ex after the first separation. Here I was. Again. It was ten years later, and I was still not loving myself and *"How did I get here?"* was still a common-thread statement in my life. I had my hunches about why I was stuck in this emotional place, but I also knew I didn't want to be there anymore. It was time to do the hard work and I was ready for it. For the next four and a half days, I threw myself into trusting the process.

On the first day, I walked into the nine-by-nine room, its walls lined with blank sheets for me to write down my emotions, and dove headfirst into the Onsite therapy world of one-on-one work with a therapist for eight hours a day. On that same day, this is what I wrote in my Onsite journal: "I want to see my worth. I want to love myself." And that was what I told my therapist I wanted to leave with. Onsite is all about experiential therapy where you in a way act out and use all the parts of your brain. You not only feel your pain, but you also get to see it and walk through it.

One day we were asked to pick a Beanie Baby to represent our inner child, who received messages throughout our childhood that colored the way we see ourselves. My therapist asked me to place my inner child in the corner of the room, then had me start placing scarves over it. Each scarf represented a negative message: "I'm bad." "I'm the problem." "No one will love me." "I'll never be enough." "It was my fault." "I'm not lovable or chosen." "Abuse is okay." "I deserved it." "I deserve abuse." "I need to be loved by a man to be worthy." "I'm not safe." As I finished laying the last scarf on my inner child, I couldn't see her anymore.

My inner child was completely covered up with all those messages. What I learned is that all this time I had been holding on to shame. I always thought My Ex was the one with the shame because of what he did wrong in our marriage. Here is the difference. Shame is "I am . . ."—a false statement you believe about yourself, a lie about who you are. Guilt is acknowledging you did something wrong. I had been confusing guilt and shame for years, never thinking I had shame because in my mind I didn't do anything wrong. Just like that, the word "shame" took on new meaning and I realized I had been walking around with shame for thirty-plus years. I thought about all these messages weighing me down, blocking my vision, and making believe things about myself that ultimately were not true or fair at all. I then imagined my daughter in this moment. I would never want her to have these feelings or carry the shame of messages that aren't hers.

I realized I had abandoned my inner child a long time ago. I didn't love her like I would my own daughter or my friends. I buried her in shame messages and let her believe that's who she was. What are the messages you have been holding on to about yourself? Who were you before the world told you any different?

The nights I was there, I had every intention to journal and read a book, or even write some of this book, but after sitting in that room and doing the hardest work I've ever done, I was tired. I wanted to be around the community of people that were feeling the same. After all we weren't allowed to have technology, so we were forced to communicate and be present, what they call a "technology detox." Not having my phone made me anxious for the first day and night. By the end of the stay, I didn't want my phone back. That's how much I loved not having it. It felt great. On the first night, a few of the community members asked me to play cornhole, and within ten minutes I felt like my authentic self. Since leaving Onsite, I've come to realize how much time I spent mindlessly on my phone, and how doing that almost numbed my feelings.

Another thing I like about Onsite is people don't know who you are. You aren't supposed to talk about what you do or who you are. You are just meant to be you. And that's exactly who I got to be. I got to be my old and true self, Jana from Michigan, and it felt so damn good. I was making friends who saw who I was for me, not what I do, or because I'm

"Jana Kramer." When I was there, I learned something that surprised me. Within the first two minutes of conversation, the question "What do you do?" is asked. At Onsite, there was no "What do you do?" We were just ourselves. Now I am more intentional with conversations, allowing others to be who they are without the attachment of what they do.

When I wasn't in my individual therapy center, we would all come together for lunch, dinner, and nighttime activities. We were united through struggle and lifted each other up with praise for the hard work, for the way God was moving in all of us. I felt God's presence come alive the night before I left. A few of the guys had some guitars, and I asked if anyone knew how to play "What a Beautiful Name." We went to church for the next three minutes. We were all singing the lyrics and praising that God took what the enemy meant for evil and turned it to good. One of the women who were there at the end wiped away a tear and said, "Thank you." We looked at her, and she said, "I haven't been able to listen to a worship song for years because I'm so angry at the church and this is the closest I've ever felt to God, and it didn't make me feel unsafe." We all had a good cry that night.

· · ·

Beyond the experiential work that we did there, I was also able to do adventure therapy. As my therapist and the adventure therapist walked to the woods, I thought to myself, "Oh Lord, what am I going to have to do?" I was just praying it had nothing to do with heights as I am afraid of that to my core. We then walked up to a forty-five-foot-high pole. I was staring my fear right in the face. The adventure therapist went on to explain that we would tack up all my negative belief messages written on sticky notes on this pole. I would climb up the pole rung by rung. Along the way, I would throw down the negative sticky note and replace the old message with the new one. I would throw away the lie and replace it with the truth. She told me it didn't matter how high I climbed, that whatever I did was going to be based on my comfort level and my journey.

I looked at her and thought, "You obviously don't know how competitive I am."

At the top, there was a small platform just big enough for my feet. I thought to myself, *"I'm going to make it all the way up and stand on there."* That was the goal that I set for myself. Let me remind you all that one time when I filmed *One Tree Hill* in Park City, I screamed the entire way up the ski lift. That's how terrified of heights I am. We were in the middle of filming a scene for the season seven finale, and I looked over to Stephen Colletti, who was riding with me, and I started to take off my clothes. And not because I wanted to jump Stephen's bones, but because I was having an anxiety attack and I couldn't breathe. I was trying to take off the twenty layers of clothing that were keeping me warm. The poor guy had no idea what was happening, but then I buried my head into his chest and yelled, "Cut!" We were able to film the scene, but it wasn't my best work to say the least, as I was clutching to the side of the lift.

Now there I was, attached to a carabiner, making my way

up the pole. When I would see a sticky note with something like, "I'm not enough," I would throw it down and say the new message, "I am enough," and so on, all the way up the pole. I stopped about twenty feet up and looked down. Big mistake. My heart started to jump out of my chest, and I felt my throat close. I kept going, finding a climbing mount to boost me higher, but my pace started to get slower. When I got to the top of the pole, I was hugging it like my life depended on it. I started to ask questions like, *"Are you sure you got me?" "If I let go, what will happen?" "Am I going to die if I let go?"* I was so scared to just let go. I debated my next steps. I was either going to let go and fall off, or I was going to make it to the top and stand on the shaky small platform. I couldn't do it. I couldn't take another step. I justified not being able to stand on the platform by acknowledging that I got to the top—then, I lowered myself by climbing down each rock-climbing mount until I made it to the bottom.

My therapist looked at me and she said, "Are you happy with what you did?"

I started off by saying I was, that it felt good to release those messages and that I was proud I made it to the top. That was true, but I wanted to do it again. I needed to do it again. I held myself back. I told myself I couldn't do it when I got up there, and back down I went. I knew it was almost time for lunch, so a part of me didn't want to hold my therapist and the guide back, but I knew I would regret it if I didn't try one more time. I needed to take that last leap for myself.

So, I said, "Jackie, can I please actually do that again?"

She looked at me like she was waiting for me to say that.

Her eyes lit up. "Yes!"

I raced up the poll, grabbing the rocks like it was easy this time, until I got back to the same spot where I got stuck before. I thought, *"Shit, here I am again."*

If that wasn't a metaphor for my life, I don't know what was. I then heard Jackie yelling words of encouragement from my Queendom, from God, from my grandpa. She asked me in the beginning of our time together who the people that speak truth into me are, that show me love—and I had them in my corner with me the entire time there. Now Jackie was speaking life into them, into me. I didn't know how it was going to be possible to get on this tiny platform, but I knew there had to be a way, and I wasn't going down until I chose myself and broke free.

I managed to get my left knee on there and then my right, my left foot and then my right. I had two feet planted on the platform. All I had to do was stand up. Honestly, at that moment I thought I was going to black out. My body felt weightless. I said this prayer: "God, please give me the strength to stand up and love myself." I then slowly started to rise and there I was, standing atop that pole—just God and me. I stood up there with so much pride and a new sense of self. I did it. I chose myself. I fought for myself.

I yelled down, "I'm ready to let go."

Instead of climbing down like I did the first time, I let go and jumped off the platform into the air. Jackie and I embraced with the most tearful hug and joyful "Fuck yeahs." That was one of the first moments of my life when I was ever truly proud of myself. It felt amazing. I realized in doing that

187

exercise, all the times I have held myself back from things I've wanted to do because I was too afraid. I also realized I couldn't let go because of what I believed about myself, who I thought I was. The shame messages.

• • • •

You are not meant to hold and carry shame and once I realized what shame really was, I was able to let go and love myself better. Another exercise my therapist made me do was write down on rocks all my shame messages that I believed. Then I had to put them in a backpack and carry them to a stream. The mile-long journey to the stream carrying that heavy pack on my back was a metaphor for everything I've been carrying most of my life. I have never felt something heavier. My body hurt. My muscles ached. Carrying those shame messages was wreaking havoc on my body.

When we got to the stream, I started to place the rocks one by one in the water. When I would place a rock, I would speak truth to it like I did at the pole. When I read the rock "I'm not worthy," I would say, "I am worthy." I didn't deserve it. I don't need a man to define my worth. I am lovable. I am safe. When I got to the rock "I deserve abuse," I took a long pause. As you have read in this book, I have struggled for years with thinking I deserved abuse. From my upbringing to my abuser, to fighting back thinking I deserved the hit. It has been a long-standing belief for me. I stared at the rock and tears started to roll down my cheeks. I said out loud, "I deserve abuse." Tears started to flow harder, and I was having a hard time saying the positive message back. The truth. Jackie saw me struggling and said, "Take deep breaths and take all the time you need." Then something came over me. I threw the rock so hard into the stream that my shoulder almost went with it. I screamed as loud as I could, "I don't deserve abuse—it's not my fault," and I then started to throw the rocks as hard as I could. After I threw the last rock, I fell to my knees and let go of thirty years of shame. Shame is a lie saying you aren't enough, and you are believing the lie that you aren't. When did you start believing those lies? What shame are you holding on to? Write them down on a rock and throw them into a river or a body of water that can wash those messages away and release them. These messages aren't yours to hold or carry. Speak truth into who you are. What you are.

Dr. Dan Allender says it best. "When the stronger parts of us care for the broken parts of us, redemption starts to happen." Speak truth into yourself. Speak life into yourself. Think about yourself as a little girl or boy. Would you want them carrying all of this? Of course not. No matter what someone said to you or spoke into you, you are not that person. Here's a prayer I like to say, perhaps it can help you: "God help me to see the things that I need to let go of to continue my growth. Help me walk away from what's comfortable and known into the unknown and what I can't see or predict."

Something else that was helpful for me to release shame was the acknowledgment that it might come up again from time to time. I wish it was like a switch where I said, "Oh great, I released it into a stream, I'm shame free." Unfortunately, it doesn't work like that. That's the hardest part about doing the work. You think to yourself, *"Well, I've done some hard things, so why am I still thinking about it and feeling this way?"* Remember, it's going to take time to unlearn everything you have learned and retrain your brain to believe different messages about yourself. If you start a new relationship and the person leaves you, you might go back to thinking, *"I'm not good enough."* What you do at that moment is where the work comes in. Instead of believing that lie and shame message, shift back to what you know in the present moment. You *are* good enough. Even if the breakup hits some core feelings about some of your old beliefs, it doesn't define your work. Remember the truths. Write them on your mirror if that will help and give yourself some grace that releasing these shame messages isn't going to happen overnight. There is no magic bullet, but two-degree shifts over time create monumental change.

Gift

"For I know the plans I have for you."

—JEREMIAH 29:11

May

The end of something is always the beginning of something greater. In May, I could acknowledge that I had walked through fire but was starting to come out the other side. I was stepping into a new Jana, and I loved who I was becoming. I started to explore and have fun and to date in more healthy ways. I didn't rush into things. I gave myself time to figure out what I liked and what I didn't and I was honest in situations where I might have just conformed to my partner in dating relationships in the past.

I could feel myself starting to thrive. For once, I was happy not being in a relationship because my journey of finding happiness in myself was actually a real thing and not something that I was just trying on. It was actually me.

I explored in a way I never had before. A year ago I had been so depressed, but this summer I was daydreaming about all the things I could do and see. It was coined "hot girl summer," but not because I was dating left and right. In fact, I promised myself and my tribe that I wouldn't start a new relationship until at least the fall. Well, I beat that, because it wasn't until winter that my heart went across seas. Hot girl summer was a time to just see what I truly liked, what I didn't, and to enjoy every moment. I was alone, I dated, I laughed and danced on beaches with my friends. And I took everything that I had learned from that spring and let the truth settle into my soul and my bones—I'm worthy of it all.

*   *   *

I've looked at my new season of life as a blessing in disguise. Never did I think I would be here, right now, where I am—in a healthy, happy, peaceful place. I craved to be here, but I didn't know if I believed it would happen. How did I get here?

A few years ago, I would have been asking that question from a place of sorrow, from a fetal position from the floor of my closet, but today I can answer that from a more grateful stance. I got here by truly doing some of the hardest work and digging in more than I ever did in my past. I got here by surviving some of the most traumatic moments of my life. True sweat and tears, "I don't know how I will get through this" moments. The battles in my past made me resilient, showed me how strong I really was and my past was a setup to get me exactly where I am today. It took my whole world falling apart to find myself in the rubble and it was up to me to clean me off. The beauty there is that there is freedom to love the life God has for you.

After my visit to Onsite there was a shift that happened in my life. My friend Kristen said to me, "This new Jana is Michigan Jana." I think she means that Michigan Jana is happy, calm, and free. I'm not one to take compliments from my friends but I felt each word she said to me because I believed it too. I have had so many people that have come into my life that have taught me so many beautiful things. The irony is most of the lessons came from very painful times in my life. I am grateful for both.

We get to decide how people can or can't treat us. The reward is in the change of your point of view, when you can see enough is enough, no matter how long it takes, when you stop begging someone to treat you better. We get to live for an audience of one and take what we have learned and heal and grow.

People come into our life to teach us lessons. If you receive them with a grateful energy, you will have brighter and healthier interactions all around. You will feel better. If you live your life from a grateful stance, you will see the gifts in things, whether negative or positive. You can adapt easier and faster when things don't go your way. Instead of focusing on why a door didn't open for you, you'll move on to the next door with excitement, knowing there must have been a reason God didn't want you to open that other door. I love a common quote that I see online: "Don't worry about the people that God has removed from your life. He saw things you didn't see and conversations you couldn't hear and made moves you wouldn't make."

God's plan is always the best. Sometimes the process is painful and so hard, but don't forget that when God is silent, that's when he's doing something for you. Taking your time while you move through hard seasons will not only allow God to move mountains, but you'll be able to see with clearer eyes and appreciate it more when you are on the other side.

Believe that each interaction is yours to own and have. There are have been many variations on this general sentiment, but the version I've adopted as my motto of late is "You have one life, live it to the fullest." Gratitude is an action. If you bring it to life through every interaction in your day, I promise you, you won't be in a fetal position the next time something goes wrong or hurts, you will be grateful for what you have learned and move on. As the Jesuit priest David Steindl-Rast once wrote in his book, *Gratefulness, the Heart of Prayer*: "The root of joy is gratefulness . . . It is not joy that makes us grateful; it is gratitude that makes us joyful."

* * *

It may sound unbelievable, but I'm also grateful for my exes. I wouldn't wish those memories on my worst enemy, but I've been able to look at those experiences through grateful lenses. I've been able to stand up, dust myself off, and see that perhaps those relationships happened for me to learn something, not simply to abuse or mock me. I was able to figure out what to do with that experience. For as much as My Ex hurt me, I'm very grateful for what our relationship taught me.

There were many words shared during our marriage that I'm sure we both would love to take back, and I know we are both thankful to be on the other side of that now. I'm grateful that My Ex taught me that I could forgive. My Ex taught me that I am stronger than I ever imagined I could be. What I'm saying is my marriage to My Ex taught me how to listen to my own inner voice and not the lies. I wasn't a perfect wife and I fell short at times, but I was a loving wife and I have a lot of love to give. That doesn't come from him saying he loves me, misses me, and wants me back. I know that the words he expressed to me in times of anger and hurt weren't the truth even though I held on to each nasty word thrown at me in the moment. When I look back, I can see we were both really hurting, and we said words that we believed in ourselves to each other instead.

Today I am grateful for how far My Ex and I have come. Our love story died, but our love for our kids will always be a thread that connects us. Our job now is to show up as the best coparents we can be and treat each other with the kind of respect that we lacked for years in our marriage. The playing field isn't destroyed with bombs. We are able now to have a clean slate, and now years removed from the hurt, we can build a different relationship. The only way to do that for me was to let the hurt and years of betrayal fully go and step into the field littered with grenades and heal each piece. Holding on to that war zone would keep me from the life I not only wanted, but deserved.

When I got divorced, I got a text from my *One Tree Hill* co-star Hilarie Burton Morgan who said, "I hope you are feeling relief right now, you don't have to carry everything yourself." I remember thinking, *"Wow she is so right,"* and what a relief it truly was. Where gratitude comes in is acknowledging the relationship for what it is. For me, that looks like recognizing that we made two spectacular children, that the hardest years of my life were with him, but here I am today, still standing and fighting for myself. In a way, he set me free when he cheated again. He set me free to fight my battle with myself—and that was the fight that I had avoided my whole life. My relationship with myself is the one I neglected for years. I could sit in my sorrows and blame him for my life falling apart or I could say thank you and walk away and choose gratitude and growth to find where I lost myself along the way. I learned to hold my own hand, not to search for someone to hold mine. He also taught me what I want in a relationship moving forward and what I don't want to experience ever again.

I look back on my relationship with Seth with gratitude too. I see it as a pivotal point in my life, both relationally and emotionally. I learned so much about who I was and what I needed to change about myself to grow thanks to that relationship. I knew what I wanted from my divorce, but I didn't know how to get it. My relationship with Seth taught me that I was going to stay stuck forever in old toxic patterns if I didn't a.) get healthy and b.) get healthy. You attract what you are.

Gift

A healthy person attracts a healthy person. I was anxiously attached after my divorce and so I attracted a man who was like My Ex in many of the ways that troubled me most. Going through that same experience amplified my same issues and I hit my bottom. I realized I could continue to let myself repeat the same pattern or do something about it. It was the hard truth that opened my eyes, and I haven't looked back since.

The peace of letting the old me go and embracing the me I always was, was the ultimate light switch to chasing joy and finding myself. Now I know men in my past will never take space up in my life again and it feels damn good to know my worth and what I deserve and want. My heart hurts for who I was a few years ago begging for a man to come back. If this has been you, or is you, don't ever ask why you aren't good enough for them. They aren't good enough for *you*. I remember reading this quote online post-divorce and living for each word:

"You will dim her light, but she will shine more brightly in the dark. You will lower her expectations, but she will raise her standards. You will cause her to hate but she will find relief, release, and beauty in the breakdown. You will make her question her sanity, but she will learn to trust her own intuition better than before. You will crush her ideas of love, but she will never settle again. You will burn her world to the ground, but she will pour her heart into becoming the best person she can be. And this time, it won't be for you; it'll be for her."

The Next Chapter

What is next? Well, I certainly know what I don't want, but what *do* I want? I want to be present with my kids. I want to be there when they fall to help them get up and understand how they feel. I want to be grateful for every touch, interaction, and encounter I have. I want to live my life with love, thoughtfulness, and kindness. I want to love with every part of my heart and fight for the great love. I want to feel supported when I feel weak or hurt, and I want to support a partner through their struggles too. I want to be able to communicate my fears and be met with empathy and love, rather than hatred and defensiveness. I want a partner who sees how short life is. I want to be in a relationship where my partner and I encourage and listen to each other as well as strive to bring out the best in each other. I want respect and love and I want to give that just as much as I want to feel it. What had the last year taught me? That I deserve all of that, but that it might come in a different form than I imagined. I know that God is good, and that real love will prevail. I discovered that the beauty of life lies in striving, hoping, and having faith. I know that I am okay for today. That I can take care of myself. That the most beautiful sunsets follow the worst storms.

Conclusion

Sunsets

In July, a full calendar year after my divorce was finalized, I started to really look around. I had spent so many months working on myself, on the interior space of my life, the rooms of my soul and the foundation of my heart. Now I felt like it was time for a fresh start on the outside.

Up on a hill, a few miles down from my house, a "for sale" sign had gone up. On a whim, I walked up to the property with my friend on our evening summertime walk. We turned the corner onto the flat parcel of land intended for a new house, and my breath caught in my throat. I had never seen the Nashville sky look so inviting. A spectacular sunset, a show of baby blue, hot pink, and burnt desert orange lit up the sky.

I have loved sunsets my entire life. I am sure they are a message from God. And this one was a sure sign from God as

I have ever seen. Sunsets are a visual reminder of a day ending, a turning page. The significance that a new day is coming, but nowadays I watch them out of gratitude for all the ways I've been blessed in that day.

Building a new house was not in the plan, or the budget. But something was on fire in me about this property. The chance to restructure my life from scratch, to build something new from the ground up for my babies and me. I imagined a safe home, with a cozy fireplace and a terrific view of the sky.

Even though I would have liked to sell the house My Ex and I lived in the day I signed the divorce papers, I wanted structure and familiarity for my kids. I also needed to sit with my memories in that house for my healing journey. Now, to be standing on this hill, breathing in with more clarity and peace, felt like a God wink. It was time.

My therapist once gave me a big, white piece of construction paper and some markers. She said, "This is going to represent your acre. Your sacred space." I encourage you to try this exercise. Whether building a new house or just reworking the corners of your heart, you can incorporate this into your life. The acre is all about creating a safe place. Or I like to call it, my sacred place. While designing your acre you are the designer. You get to call the shots.

With my acre I drew my new house on the piece of paper, and then my therapist asked me how I wanted it surrounded. Did I want high walls? A gate? How did I want to feel protected? I put one of those cute horse fences and then she asked me who stays out of the gate and who gets to come in? We get to choose who comes into our space. How far is your ex allowed onto your acre? Does he get to make it into the kitchen or does he stop at the front door? What feels safe and good to you? Remember this is your space. You get to be the one who chooses those boundaries, no one else. Maybe you have set boundaries in the past but you need to change them. That's okay. People who fight against these changes are the ones you need to keep even farther away because they might not be safe for you.

She then asked me if there was a special place in my acre where no one gets to go to. A sacred space only for you or maybe those closest to you. I love a screened-in porch so for the new house I decided to build one off my master closet. This will be my sacred sanctuary to light a fire, lay on the swing, and just be me. My truest form. There are only a few people that get to sit in that space and the others can enjoy the living room and the rest of the backyard. You get to create your own acre. So what do you want yours to look like?

• • •

Years after my divorce, I've never been happier. I never thought I would say that and ever really feel that. I would always pray for happiness, but to be honest, I didn't even know what that felt like. These days, I won't settle for less. I have found authentic happiness for the first time in my life and when I truly loved myself is when I found love.

The key to happiness? I don't claim to have the key, but

what worked for me was shedding the toxic energy, the toxic relationships, and having a massive heart shift to the belief that I was worthy of the happy ending.

I started to choose me, to work on myself, and to really find out what I need and want.

I let go of everything that was not serving me.

I let go of the shame and the years of beating myself up.

I started to love to spend time with myself because I started to love who I was becoming and who I was.

I started to find new light in relationships, and to embrace every moment with a lighter and more joyful attitude.

I started to be thankful for the past because there is beauty in the struggle. There is beauty in the lessons of the last thirty-plus years.

I started to look at my life as if it were a movie and began to root for myself as a character.

I looked at my past relationships and admired the strength and courage it took pull myself together and move on.

I started to cheer myself on.

I started to celebrate all the small and happy moments by professing "I'm happy" out loud and giving myself permission to keep feeling that way.

I showed myself respect.

I was reborn after my marriage in the best way possible. Today, I am betting on myself. I always said that people put me in a box, that I had to be a certain way; ultimately, I realized the person putting me in the box was me. I was the one who held myself back from my true happiness because I didn't think I deserved any better. I didn't think it could get any better, so I kept my head down and just walked the path I had chosen.

Now, I love the woman I see because from the moment I decided to get up and not play the victim, I have been fighting for myself. I have been bringing myself back to life. I have held the key to my happiness all along. Not from a relationship, or a man. Me. So yes, you can be happy again, and you will be damn proud of the person you become when you finally turn the page.

Acknowledgments

We are not meant to walk through this life alone, and I would have never been able to get through this season or make it to the other side if it wasn't for everyone who held me up along the way.

First and foremost I want to acknowledge my Jolie and Jace. Your hearts, love, and cuddles are everything that I need and more. I am so proud to be your mommy.

To my therapist, Amy Alexander. I will never be able to thank you enough for the many hours you have spent with me over the last four years, and for the not-in-office hours when I called you from a closet. Thank you for loving me however I showed up in your room and for not giving up on me. You gave me eyes to see and strength to leave, but most important, thank you for leading me back to myself.

To Kathryn. My OG. You have fought for me for years, and

I can't think of anyone else I would want next to me through it all. Thank you for never giving up on me and loving me.

Kristen, Sara, Pamelyn, and Julie, I would have never been able to get through that first year without each and every one of you. You are all my sisters, teachers, and my strength, and I'll forever be indebted to Queendom.

To My Ex—thank you for showing me that there can be kindness and respect on the other side of a story we both didn't see going this way.

My family, thank you for your support and being there for me through it all.

My editors, Sydney Rogers and Katy Hamilton, thank you for helping me bring my story to life and for believing that I could do it.

My agent, Margaret Riley King, and HarperCollins for believing in me and giving my book a home.

To my fiancé, Allan Russell, thank you for showing me what a real love looks and feels like.

To all of you who are reading this book, thank you for supporting me throughout the years. It means more to me than you will ever know.

And lastly, to God, and my two angel grandpas. Thank you for always being there for me up in heaven and giving me the strength to keep seeing joy.

You are all my champions and I'm not only blessed but I'm grateful to do life with you and all the chapters to come.

Resources

Below is a list of books I read after my divorce, as well as some mental health and therapy resources. I loved how helpful they were during this time, and wanted to include them here if you are looking for more guidance in this area.

Disarming the Narcissist by Wendy T. Behary
The Betrayal Bond by Patrick J. Carnes
The Verbally Abusive Relationship by Patricia Evans
How to Do the Work by Dr. Nicole LePera
Begin Again by Max Lucado
Whole Again by Jason MacKenzie
The Power of Letting Go by John Purkiss
Leave a Cheater, Gain a Life by Tracy Schorn
It's Not Supposed to be Like This by Lysa Terkeurst
Forgiving What You Can't Forget by Lysa Terkeurst

Resources

A Return to Love by Marianne Williamson
Better Than Okay by Brandi Wilson

THERAPY:
Onsite workshops
The Refuge Center for Counseling
Better Help

About the Author

Jana Kramer is a country music singer and actress. She has starred in the beloved television shows *One Tree Hill*, *Friday Night Lights*, and *Dancing with the Stars*, and has released two albums: *Jana Kramer* and *Thirty One*. She is cohost of the award-winning iHeart Podcast, *Whine Down with Jana Kramer* and is also the coauthor of the *New York Times* best-selling book, *The Good Fight*. Jana lives in Nashville with her two children.